APARTMENT MANAGER'S SURVIVAL GUIDE

Lona M. Kerzman

LoDay Publications, Vancouver, Washington

APARTMENT MANAGER'S SURVIVAL GUIDE
By Lona M. Kerzman

Published by:
   LoDay Publications
   Box 2722
   Vancouver, Wa. 98668

All rights reserved. No part of this book may be reproduced or transmitted in any form or by any means, electronic or mechanical, including photocopying, recording or by any information storage and retrieval system without written permission from the author, except for the inclusion of brief quotations in a review.

Copyright © 1999 by Lona M. Kerzman
   All rights reserved

Printed in the United States of America

   Library of Congress Catalog Card Number: 99-94260

ISBN: 0-9670876-0-0

All apartment community names featured in this book are fictitious. Any similarity to real apartment communities is purely coincidental.

Table of Contents

Chapter 1:	Why Property Management?	1
Chapter 2:	Perks of the Business	4
Chapter 3:	Disadvantages of the Business	9
Chapter 4:	Answering the Ad	15
Chapter 5:	Your Resume	21
Chapter 6:	The Interview	30
Chapter 7:	Finding the Map	32
Chapter 8:	Office Atmosphere	34
Chapter 9:	Preparing Your Model	37
Chapter 10:	Smell and Other Senses	40
Chapter 11:	Showing up Early	44
Chapter 12:	Answering the Phone	46
Chapter 13:	Knowing Your Directions	50
Chapter 14:	Greeting and Standing	52
Chapter 15:	Keeping the Doors Open	54
Chapter 16:	Marketing	56
Chapter 17:	Finding out Your Customer's Needs	63
Chapter 18:	Pre-qualifying	65
Chapter 19:	Screening Services	70
Chapter 20:	Sample Agreements	76
Chapter 21:	Guest Cards	78
Chapter 22:	Give out Those Apps!	80
Chapter 23:	Accommodating Dates	82
Chapter 24:	Move-in Packets	84
Chapter 25:	Don't Take Cash!	88
Chapter 26:	Flushing 'Em Out	89
Chapter 27:	Security	92

Chapter 28:	Youth Careers	96
Chapter 29:	Sale of the Property	99
Chapter 30:	Beware the Clipboard	100
Chapter 31:	Taking Classes	102
Chapter 32:	You Never Know Who Your Next Boss Will Be	104
Chapter 33:	Newsletters	108
Chapter 34:	Creating a Festive Atmosphere	111
Chapter 35:	Staff Meetings	116
Chapter 36:	Welcome Home!	118

FORWARD

This book was born as a result of answering the question "How do I get into property management?" more times than I can account for, and the words of a C.E.O. who stated "You really need to market this!"

Twenty years of "on the job" experience, years of training and hiring managers and "marketing the unmarketable" have taught invaluable lessons. A lot of trade secrets are revealed in this publication, and it is my sincere hope that the shortcuts you learn will aid in your success should you choose to follow this career path.

WARNING—DISCLAIMER

This book is designed to provide information in regard to the subject matter covered. It is sold with the understanding that the publisher and author are not engaged in rendering legal, accounting or other professional services. If legal or other expert assistance is required, the services of a competent professional should be sought.

It is not the purpose of this manual to reprint all the information that is otherwise available to the author and/or publisher, but to complement, amplify and supplement other texts. You are urged to read all the available material, learn as much as possible about apartment management and to tailor the information to your individual needs.

Every effort has been made to make this manual as complete and as accurate as possible. However, there may be mistakes both typographical and in content. Therefore, this text should be used only as a general guide and not as the ultimate source of apartment management.

The purpose of this manual is to educate and entertain. The author and LoDay Publications shall have neither liability nor responsibility to any person or entity with respect to any loss or damage caused, or alleged to be caused, directly or indirectly by the information contained in this book.

If you do not wish to be bound by the above, you may return this book to the publisher for a full refund.

CHAPTER 1: WHY PROPERTY MANAGEMENT?

So you want a career in apartment property management (also referred to as "resident property management", the official title for this position). Good for you. It's an exciting, challenging and potentially profitable field. People are continually asking me, "How do I get into this business?" This book is designed to provide complete answers to all the questions you might have regarding this business. It will take you through a step-by-step process that will first help you make this career decision and then show you how to become a successful resident manager.

"Mom and Pop" Management. Seventeen or more years ago, "Mom and Pop" was truly the representative model of this industry. It also gave the industry a bad rap at times. Let me give you an example. My husband's and my first landlords "Jack and Lil" lived below us in our very first apartment in Las Vegas, Nevada. Lil basically ran the 30-unit apartment complex that we lived in, and well, I'm not sure what Jack did. I do know that Jack nipped a bit (I mean alcohol), because we would often hear tremendous arguing at night or even a few hard knocks against the wall—which would probably fall under our domestic dispute laws today. Anyway, in those days landlords simply took your rent money (weekly in Las Vegas, probably due to gambling concerns) and gave you the keys to your apartment. That was it. There were none of the rental agreements, notices of disturbances, etc. that we have today. Everything was verbally sealed with a handshake.

We knew we were in trouble, however, when Jack appeared at our door at 11:00 p.m. one night, after a few drinks, and asked us not to walk on the floor after 10:00 p.m. I had to explain that this was a rather difficult feat to accomplish as my husband did not get off work until midnight. Lil too became a problem, as she approached me one day returning from my job and asked me not to wear my mini-skirt home (this was the late 60's), as the older ladies were upset when I climbed the stairs. As if!!! Now, three decades later, times have changed. Hemlines have more variety, and managers have more responsibility.

For my husband and myself this career choice was easy. We had just relocated from out of state, our money was tied up in a real estate sale, our daughter was one year old, and our funds were getting low. We were definitely motivated! We had sent out letters (no resumes then) in response to a number of want-ads soliciting managers, and finally we received a call from a retired "colonel" who managed a property management firm. After a brief conversation he hired us over the phone, sight unseen. No interview, no background or reference check. Just drive by and if we wanted the job it was ours. We drove into the new 90-unit complex, looked around, and wondered "What do we do with all these apartments?" But we accepted, met the "colonel," picked up paperwork and keys, and moved in the next day. To make matters worse, they had an "open house" advertised in the paper for that week-end. He wished us luck and said he would see us Monday.

This kind of occurrence is rare these days, but if it should happen to you, this book is designed to help you survive. Our first lessons, shortcuts and solutions came as a result of this experience. Many lessons would follow. Well, we have come a long way since those days. Tenants these days are referred to as "residents" not "tenants" and they have rights. Some of these rights seem legitimate—others you could argue about. We now have enough paperwork to make buying a home a piece of cake by comparison. So familiarity with the laws and the paperwork is a must. Resident management is a daily adventure. You will meet fascinating people, learn invaluable business skills, and you may have the time of your life. It is not for everyone. Reading this book will help you decide if it is for you—and it will outline everything you need to know to be an effective manager. Enjoy the ride!

CHAPTER 2: Perks of the Business

Let's start with some of the good news. There are a number of perks.

Rent Allowance. This is one of the best parts of the job. Because in many cases you are required to live on-site, an apartment is provided for you. Many managers forget to include the value of this perk when they consider the salary. With increasingly higher rents these days, up to $1500 per month, don't forget to include this in your calculations when you consider the job. Also, as of this publication, rent is not considered taxable income if you are required to live on-site. So when you file with the IRS, you do not have to declare it as taxable.

Utilities. Many owners pay your utilities. These can be quite costly, therefore quite a savings to you. Water, sewer, and garbage are almost always provided free to residents in apartment communities therefore you have that benefit. And your electric bill may be paid as well, leaving you free of utility expenses.

Cable T.V. Cable television companies offer free cable to managers and many times free movie channels. The reason for this is that you provide leads of new move-ins to cable personnel, and you also provide service to their technicians should they need access to an apartment. Years ago, managers needed to let cable people into every apartment, so we really earned this perk. But thank goodness, with technology, we have gotten away from most of this time-consuming service.

Newspapers. Many companies provide a daily newspaper so that staff can keep abreast of the rental market. With specials continually offered, and rent rates frequently changing, you need to know who your competition is and what they're offering. Newspapers also give you a good way to know what is happening in the community, new business coming into the area, as well as the current events.

With these perks alone, you can already see that most of your daily living expenses are paid for.

Gas Allowance. Company owners will usually reimburse managers for mileage, either in the form of a set allowance (such as $50 per month), or on a per mile basis (such as $.28 per mile) to cover your expense of using your vehicle for picking up maintenance supplies, office supplies, etc. The only way this would not apply is if a company pick-up or vehicle were provided, in which case you would have a vehicle to drive at work. Another perk is that, living on-site, you save yourself transportation costs to and from work, and the hassle of morning traffic.

Carports, Garages, Storage. If the property has these amenities, you are generally provided one or all of these for your vehicle and belongings.

Phones, Beepers, Cell Phones. Telephones are rarely if ever offered as a perk, as many an employer has been left with the final long distance bill of a disgruntled employee. However, a beeper is generally provided so that you can be reached in case of an emergency. An answering service or at minimum an answering machine is usually provided so you can leave your home or beeper number in case of emergency. Occasionally, depending on the size of the property a cell phone may be provided.

Medical. Almost all companies provide complete medical and dental insurance coverage. Dependents are extra.

Retirement. Our experience has shown few companies provide this benefit. However, we currently work for one that does. After seven years, we are fully vested.

Vacation. The industry standard is one week after the first year; two weeks after two years; and a maximum three weeks after three years.

Education. Most companies pay for all property management-related education, seminars, and training sessions. Property management is one of the few remaining industries where with little or no formal education, you can start at an entry level and work your way up to the highest management position.

Flexible Hours. Since you are salaried, it is easy to schedule doctor and dentist appointments, lunch engagements, etc. at your convenience. You will end up making up the time as there will be occasions when you have to work past office hours or will answer a night call.

Working with your spouse. This may or may not be an advantage. It depends on your relationship. Some couples simply cannot work together. Others complement each other perfectly. Many companies have gotten away from teams, due to the fact that one person performs well and the other person does not, which creates havoc. If you are hired as a team, generally one handles the office and leasing duties, and the other is the maintenance. If you're hired as a single manager, you will most likely have a leasing agent or assistant manager and a maintenance person on staff.

Childcare. You will be able to spend quality time with your children. As your office is on-site near your home, you will be readily available. Some smaller properties have their office attached to the home, which if you have smaller children works very well. With the increasingly expensive price of childcare, this is an excellent benefit.

Extra income potential. Besides your monthly salary, there are occasionally opportunities to earn extra income. Owners of properties sometimes pay managers extra for painting and cleaning vacant apartments, rather than hiring this work out. This is usually paid by the hour. If the property should have a laundry room, managers are usually paid a monthly amount for maintaining these facilities, which in turn helps pay your laundry expenses if your apartment does not come furnished with a washer and dryer.

Bonuses. Some management firms or owners pay

extra for meeting or exceeding occupancy, income, expense and net operating income levels. New properties (referred to as lease-ups) often offer commissions for each new lease. Managers may qualify as well as leasing agents.

Positive acknowledgment for your work. The physical condition of your property is available for the community and your employer to see at all times. For those who are good at what they do, you as well as your staff will reap the rewards.

As you can see, there are many benefits to being a resident manager. Some come in the form of perks, some are opportunities, and some represent a savings to you. Especially if you are people-oriented, you may find that this is your job of choice.

CHAPTER 3: DISADVANTAGES OF THE BUSINESS

As with any business, there are disadvantages. So let's look at the downside portion.

Night calls. You are at times on-call at night. Hopefully, you have additional staff besides yourself to share this with you and trade off nights. Many properties have answering services that will screen your calls and refer only the emergency ones to you, but you are at the mercy of the operator who may be inexperienced and underpaid, and to this person a broken garbage disposal is an emergency. You at the very least will want an answering machine to screen your calls, or else you may find yourself working 24 hours a day. If you have a pager, include the number on your answering machine message to have residents call in case of emergency. They can then either leave a detailed message if you have voice mail or input their phone number for you to call them back.

Let's define emergency. Technically, emergency calls in this industry are fire, flood, or police emergency—and nothing else. Few residents have these emergencies, and to them the smallest inconvenience is an emergency. It is almost as if the apartment manager is a hotel/motel manager. Here is where you need to educate your residents. Whether in person when you move them in, or in print in monthly newsletters, do take the time to educate them. Most calls can be taken care of during regular business hours. You will occasionally get calls regarding loud parties after 10:00 p.m. when the city noise ordinance takes effect. You will have to check on this. If it is truly a loud party, you will need to contact the resident and tell him or her to hold it down—either in person or by phone, in which case you will need to look up the phone number. Hopefully you have an up-to-date list of resident phone numbers. You will find little help from the police department with parties; in fact they will tell residents to contact the manager. You should follow up this party the next day with a "Notice of Disturbance." If one unit accumulates three notices, you should consider evicting the resident, as he or she is clearly a nuisance not only to you but the entire neighborhood. I'll discuss the eviction process later. Under NO circumstances should you try to handle a domestic dispute. They are the most dangerous not only to you, but to the police department. In fact, on domestic calls, police do not come alone, but bring back-up cars with them. Call the police, and always follow this type of call up the next day with the Notice of Disturbance. Unfortunately, these calls are more common today than a few years ago, and they occur in all walks of life. There is no way to know who falls into this pattern when you rent to them, so don't blame yourself, but do take corrective action. The majority of your night calls will be complaints that a stereo or television is too loud. With technology moving as fast as it has, this has become more of a problem, especially with surround sound, etc. Most people respond well to a polite request to turn down the volume, and you seldom have to repeat the visit.

Staff. There is generally speaking a high turnover in staff in this industry. Most non-managerial jobs are entry level, and as such receive entry-level wages. Therefore you spend considerable time interviewing, hiring and occasionally firing people. One way to encourage personnel to stay with the job even with the lower wage scale is to emphasize the long-term advantages of working their way up, possibly to management within your company or another. You can also point out to them that this experience will be valuable even in other fields of work.

Keeping the door open. You do have to be open every day, and if one of your staff members is sick, you may have to work. One positive aspect of this is that it earns you a day off later (although, if you are too busy to take a day off, it doesn't help much). If you are sick, that can be a problem, especially if you do not work with a partner. If there is absolutely no alternative, you may have to close and resort to emergency phone messages, keeping the phone close by.

Stress. With any job there comes stress. You will have residents to deal with every day. Most times their problems are minor and could be readily solved by themselves, yet they will look to you to solve them. A word of caution. NEVER get involved in people's private lives, marital troubles, or gossip of any kind. This is extremely dangerous. You will have to use your skills as a mediator between neighbors, and you will further develop these skills, I guarantee it. You will have to solve late rent payment problems (remember that it is a business and not a personal issue). Be firm, but fair. You will also have deadlines, and reports that have to be sent into the owner or corporate company. You'll need to always mark your calendar to remind yourself of these. It is very embarrassing to have forgotten an important report. In fact, I believe my most useful tool is my desk calendar where I can write down important notes a month at a time.

Working with your spouse. Remember I said this could be an advantage, or a disadvantage. Some couples can live together but not work together. Sometimes, I think the reason is, we don't treat our spouse with as much respect as we would an employee. We wouldn't yell at our employee for some minor infraction, but we do yell at our spouse, and this seems quite natural at times. In the work place respect is essential. If you need to argue, do it at home, away from the employees' eyes and ears. Air your grievance and work toward a solution. Sometimes couples just cannot work together, and if this is the case it will become clear to you. Don't feel bad about it, just accept it, and find an alternative solution. Perhaps one member of the team can work elsewhere, and one can manage. It will become clear whether this business is for you or not.

Responsibility. There is a lot of responsibility. Sometimes I compare it to being the mayor of a small town. You are the head of however many apartments you have, and however many people. That is responsibility. You have a key to every one of their apartments, and you must guard that pass key with your life. You can take no chance on losing it or letting it fall into the wrong hands. You have situations every day that you can't let slide due to the consequences. You have bosses to answer to, owners to answer to, residents to answer to. You must make decisions, and right or wrong stand with them. You cannot be indecisive. If you take responsibility seriously, these concerns will not be a problem.

Loss of privacy. Unfortunately, though you guard your apartment address from residents, some invariably find you and will come to your door. Staff will too, though they hate to bother you. So you do give up some right to privacy. A common problem is residents being locked out because they forgot or lost their keys. A good way to curb this is to institute a "Lock-out Charge," say of $25.00 between the hours of 10:00 p.m. and 8:00 a.m. It's funny how residents find solutions to this problem when they have to pay a fee up front to get let into their apartment. We justify this policy with the explanation that we have to pay staff to open their apartments after business hours. This usually stops the grumble. Lock-outs decrease by 99 per cent with this policy in effect, and you get some sleep.

CHAPTER 4: ANSWERING THE AD

Now that you have an understanding of resident property management and have examined all the positive and negative sides to this career choice, your next step is to answer the ad.

Even if you do not have experience directly related to property management, apply. If the interview goes well, you may be hired for an entry-level position. If you have any management or supervisory experience in another business field, this is definitely to your advantage. You will want to make note of it in your cover letter as well as your resume.

First, you have to find the section of the classified ads that advertise for these positions. They are not all listed in the same column or under the same capital letter as you would think. I mention this because my husband and I have sometimes found ads in the strangest places. So knowing where to look is going to eliminate the possibility that you might miss the job of your dreams. First, look under "A" for "Apartment Managers." You will also find listed "Assistant Managers," Maintenance positions at apartment complexes, Leasing positions, etc. All these are listed under "A" as they pertain to apartment management.

Next, look under "M" for "Managers." Some firms or private owners who don't know that they should be specific in their ad will use the term "Manager."

Third, look under "P" for "Property Managers."

Some firms call their on-site managers "property managers." You will need to read these ads carefully to check whether a position is for an on-site or an in-house property manager.

Last, look for display ads. Our finest position came from a display ad which looked totally out of place, but we answered it anyway, and it truly was a job to die for. Read through the ads. There are so many variances to these jobs that you will really need to sort through them. Some ads want "team only," which with new laws can mean male and female, female and female, male and male. All are eligible to apply. Other ads list "Manager" wanted. Generally, these mean a single person, but if you're a couple, you have nothing to lose by applying anyway. In the past, most firms chose to hire only teams, or couples, but the market has shifted increasingly to single managers, with separate maintenance positions and leasing positions. However, this can still work well for a couple, as one person can accept the management position and reap all the benefits of on-site management, while the other works at a separate position.

Now that you have selected which ads you want to answer, you are ready to "sell yourself." You are your own best salesperson, and this is your opportunity to do so, in your resume and cover letter. Don't be afraid to come out and say, in plain and direct language, what things you do well.

Most ads will list Post Office boxes, so allow two to

three weeks to hear back. Make sure that you have an answering machine for when you are not home, and also list on your resume an alternate phone number where you can be reached. If an employer cannot reach you, he or she will simply go on to another application.

In some ads, you will find a phone number listed. Usually, this means either the community is very small, or it is an owner advertising, or someone is in a real hurry to hire! You will want to check these out of course, and an interview can be set up rather quickly on these ads.

Once you hear back from the management firm or owner, they will want to set up an interview with you. Here is where I believe it pays to be somewhat assertive but, of course, polite. You could be wasting your time as well as theirs, so I am going to list some basic questions for you to ask to make sure you both qualify. If an employer does not respect this, then I suggest that you do not want to work for him or her anyway. All questions here are phrased as for a couple. If you're a single individual, you would of course modify them accordingly.

Question one. Are we required to live on-site? Occasionally, this is not required, but most times it is.

Question two. Is one position for office work and the other for maintenance?

Question three. What is the salary? Very important question. The answers to this will vary greatly. We used to be able to "ballpark" $10 per unit. The ability to estimate has long disappeared. Some salaries are high for small properties, and low for large properties, so there is no way other than to ask. When you do ask, make sure you get clarification. Sometimes an employer will say "$1,000 per month", but neglect to tell you that you have to pay $600 rent out of that amount. This is the exception, rather the norm, but it would be an unpleasant surprise, so ask for that clarification. Do you mean $1,000 plus free rent? Is there medical and dental insurance paid? Are utilities included or do we pay them? Is there a gas allowance? Who pays the phone? Have a list of your financial questions ready, and run down the list as you speak to your prospective employer. No question is dumb, and it's better to be safe than sorry. You don't want to go through the trauma of another move, just because you didn't get all the information at the interview.

Question four. What are the hours? Do you have week-ends off? Do we have relief for these days off? Many properties use answering services and you can end up on call 24 hours a day if you are not careful. What exactly is your relief? Very important! You will "burn out" very quickly if you do not have relief. What is the personal leave policy as well as vacation policy?

Question five. Where is the property located? If it is in a crime-infested part of the city, then that definitely is not for you. How many apartments will you manage? What is the clientele like?

Question six. How many employees operate the property? What are your responsibilities? Does the company use outside vendors for cleaning and painting?

Question seven. How soon do you need someone to start? If it is tomorrow, be prepared. It happens that way sometimes.

After you have asked these questions, do not turn down the position immediately, just because it does not fully meet with your expectations. Perhaps it is a large firm with lots of future opportunities, so you may want to take the opportunity to get "your foot in the door." Or maybe this is not the greatest job, but if it's tolerable you can move on to another position once you have proven yourself. So think twice before you say no. An associate once said to me, "If you're going to burn bridges, you might as well blow them up." She was right.

The next chapter is on how to write a resume. To some of you this might seem minor or unimportant. But if you had met as many people as I have who do not apply for jobs they desperately want because they don't know how, you'd understand why I feel this is important. And if you already have a resume, one you're happy with—well, it's still possible you might find a tip for improving it.

Chapter 5: Your Resume

Most companies require a resume, even for minor positions. Unfortunately, most people do not have a resume handy when an opportunity presents itself.

Many people are afraid of the word "resume" and will simply walk away from this task. They feel they would not have a clue how to write a resume. That is why this chapter is included. You might not know that there are professional services which do nothing but write resumes for people, so if all else fails, you can always go this route, but it really is not that hard. A resume is a form letter in essence that tells about you, your strong points, your work experience, and even sometimes something personal. Having been on both sides, having sent in a million resumes to employers, and having been also on the other side receiving a million resumes, I am in a position to give you some useful advice on this. Here is the best approach to use, in my opinion.

First, it is should be one page only. I have thrown away more resumes that were book length than I can remember. I do not have time, nor does any employer have time, to read your life story. If it is that good, sell your story. You can say everything that needs to be known on one page. Be brief and concise.

Second, attach a "cover letter" to the front of your resume. This can actually be more important that the resume itself. You may not believe this, but it is true.

Personality comes through in a cover letter, in a way that does not in the resume. This is your time to "shine." Tell a little about yourself and why you want this position. This part may in fact tell all an employer needs to know. Many times property managers train their own staff, so they are not so much looking for experience, as someone who seems honest, reliable and able to deal with people. A word of caution. Do not hype yourself. People see through this. The plain truth is the best policy.

Third, type both the cover letter and the resume. If you do not have a typewriter or computer, go to the library or borrow from a friend. Never hand write. More papers are thrown away simply because employers cannot read the handwriting or incorrect English is used. You must be able to communicate in this business, and poor English will come through in a hand written resume.

Fourth, make sure that you put your phone number on both the cover letter and the resume, as sometimes paperwork does become separated. Also, enclose a message number if possible.

Last, make a master resume for yourself and, if applicable, your partner. If you have a computer, it will be easy to update it in the future. If you do not have a computer, type a master resume with no address or phone number listed. Make lots of copies. Then when you need a resume in a hurry, simply type on one of the copies the phone number and address that applies. I learned about this from past experience. More than once I have had to retype my resume because we moved, and it is not a fun project to keep redoing it. People's addresses and phone number change, often in some cases, and if you have copies, you can simply add the information when needed. Keep in mind that you will need to update your resume as the years go by, as your experience increases. Even so, I still work from a resume typed for me twenty years ago when I desperately needed one and did not know how to write one. It still works today, and I am still grateful to the person who designed it for me. This is my way of giving back, to share samples of the resumes created for us, in hopes that they will be of help to you.

Before, going over the resume, I want to give you an example of a "cover letter."

August 18, 1998

Dave & Lona Kerzman
2112 N.E. Pine Lane
Vancouver, Wa. 98662 (360)222-0055
Message:(360)461-4256

To Whom it may Concern;

My husband and I are mailing our resumes to you regarding the position advertised in the *Newsdaily* newspaper.

We are recently relocated to this area to be near family and are seeking employment in Vancouver.

Our experience includes 20 years of managing up to 400 apartments. We have extensive experience in all phases of property management, including marketing, maintenance, pool care, as well as landscaping.

If you have any questions, please do not hesitate to call.

Thank you for your consideration. We look forward to hearing from you.

Sincerely,

Dave & Lona Kerzman

Dave & Lona Kerzman

As you can see the letter is brief, but tells why you are seeking employment (to be near family). It also gives a brief overview of your experience (the resume tells the rest). I think it is important to invite employers to call if they have questions or concerns, and remember to thank them in advance for taking the time to look over your resume. Don't forget to sign your name in the area after Sincerely.

On the envelope make sure you list your return address in case of any errors or the possibility that the listing is out of date.

Lona M. Kerzman
2112 N.E. Pine Lane
Vancouver, Wa. 98662
(360) 222-0055 Message (360)461-4256

OBJECTIVE

To utilize management and public-relations skills to contribute to the overall efficiency and operation of a growth-oriented organization.

SUMMARY OF QUALIFICATIONS

Management: 20 years experience in real estate property management including on-site for property management firms, as well as directly for owner. Extensive experience in landlord-tenant law; direct operations of large communities up to 400 units.

Public Relations: Proven ability to deal with employees, the public, professional organizations and clients.

Communications: Computer experienced, good overall communications skills via correspondence, telephone, or in person while maintaining friendly, yet professional manner.

Personal: Family-oriented, dependable, honest and caring; consistently follows through with assignments;

able to adjust to a wide variety of duties and responsibilities.

WORK EXPERIENCE

Quantum Residential: Manager 200 apartment homes. Responsibilities include staff supervision, budgeting, banking, weekly and monthly computer reports, invoicing, promotion, overall operations.

J.G. Jones Company: Manager 260 apartments. Supervised staff of 7 to create team atmosphere with the objective to maximize profits while keeping expenses to minimum. Extensive marketing, promotion, advertising, establishing landlord-tenant relations.

Rolling Hills Townhouses: Manager. Property manager responsible to owner for 88 townhomes. Duties included leasing, banking, rent collection, establishing an accounting system, scheduling maintenance, general management duties.

Previous experience: Area representative for Portland investors supervising 5 Eugene-Springfield complexes. Manager 343-unit luxury community in Lake Oswego; including overseeing new construction and lease-up of 2 new phases apartment homes.
Property Manager. Management of 470 homes for local banks.

References upon request.

David R. Kerzman
2112 N.E. Lane
Vancouver, Wa. 98662
(360) 222-0055 Message (360) 461-4256

OBJECTIVE

To utilize extensive maintenance and management skills in a full-time position with a service oriented organization.

SUMMARY OF QUALIFICATIONS

PROBLEM SOLVING: Progressive, self-starting, task oriented, high achiever, with proven competence in solving mechanical, electrical, plumbing and structural problems.

MAINTENANCE: Extensive maintenance skills to include major appliance repair, plumbing, electrical, carpeting and vinyl installation, pool maintenance, landscaping, and locksmith.

MANAGEMENT: 20 years property management experience to include all aspects of apartment management, staff supervision and problem solving.

WORK EXPERIENCE

QUANTUM MANAGEMENT: Manager 200 apartment homes. Duties include staff supervision, pool/spa care, turnovers, purchasing, general management.

J.G. JONES COMPANY: Manager 260 units. Supervised maintenance staff of 3. Oversaw operations to include personnel employment and supervision, payroll.

D&L MAINTENANCE. {Self-Employed}Business Maintenance. All facets apartment and home maintenance including plumbing, electrical, vinyl repair and installation.

PREVIOUS EXPERIENCE: Plumbing sales, industrial parts sales and service, hotel management, construction.

References upon request.

CHAPTER 6: THE INTERVIEW

 This is the most important part of your job search. After your resume has reached the prospective employer and you have been called for an interview, it's time to prepare. Having been on both sides of the fence, having been hired numerous times, as well as having hired many people for these positions, this is my game plan. I've got it down.

 Sex. Now that I have your attention, I'll explain how this process is a little sexist. If you are applying for a team position (we'll assume male and female, for this example), I sincerely recommend that the female pull out all the stops. Dress to kill! That is, make sure your grooming is immaculate and you look like a million bucks. Your knowledge too will be taken into consideration, but not so much as your presentation of yourself. You are selling your confident, professional self. The reason here is that you represent the person who will be dealing with the residents, as well as drawing the kind of clientele that you represent. If you dress as a 60's love child, you will probably draw 60's love children as your residents. (No offense intended, as I myself come from the 60's.) You probably will not know what property you are interviewing for at the time of the interview, so best to play safe. You can always downscale your image if necessary, but you never get a second chance to make a first impression. Now here is where the difference lies. If the other partner is a male, you are most likely to scare off any employer if you come dressed to kill in a business suit. They will probably think you have your eye on their job (which is actually threatening). Employers assume you are the maintenance part of the team. Your skills will be more important than your clothes in this case. They want to know you are not afraid of a little hard work. The best choice here (unless it is the Ritz and you know this) is a pair of jeans and a shirt, no tie and of course impeccable grooming. If it is a one-person position, the lady would keep to the same standard; the male in this case would perhaps go with more of a khaki pant, semi-professional attire.

Present a positive image. Any customer service skills and maintenance experience should be brought to the employer's attention. You are your own salesperson. Who better than you to promote yourself? But don't overkill; be somewhat humble. Remember also to be excited! The property you are offered may not be exactly what you had in mind, but take lemons and make lemonade. The point is to get hired with the company and make yourself invaluable. Then the next property offered to you may be the one of your dreams. Good luck!

CHAPTER 7: Finding the Map

Now that you have been hired to your new property, let's start with the basics.

You cannot direct people to your property if you don't know where you live! You take a piece of paper and write down directions from all areas of town until you get used to giving them out. Use landmarks wherever possible. Examples: next to hospital, close to community college, etc.

Speaking of maps—when you are hired to a property, the first thing upon arriving, find the site plan. Most times when you start at a job, you are simply handed the keys and wished a lot of luck! You may not know where apartment B-17 is located. Humor is important here, as when you haven't had time to locate the apartment you simply say, "I have no idea, but you'll love it!" Never underestimate humor, it will bail you out many times. A site map is very handy at times like this. I like to make a small clip-board size copy to carry with me, and as I am chatting away with my prospective resident I am really frantically searching for B-17!

Check for maps and plans with locations of water shut-offs, in case of an emergency such as a water line break.

It is a good idea also to locate apartment keys in advance. They are almost always guaranteed to be mixed up, until you use your organizational skills to straighten them out. It is also embarrassing to give out keys and have your resident return five minutes later saying they won't open the door. You'll also want to try out all the pass keys you are given (most of which belong to nothing), so that you have handy access in case of emergency, and also so you can open the door to that vacant apartment.

Also, get to know how your office equipment works. The typewriter, the copier, the fax machine, the telephone. This may sound silly, but many simple things can be very complicated, especially if you aren't given much time to learn them, and this is almost always the case. When managers are hired, it should have happened two or three weeks before, but of course it didn't because they didn't meet you, the perfect match, yet.

CHAPTER 8: OFFICE ATMOSPHERE

Atmosphere! The most important element to your office and/or recreation center. Spend a lot of time developing this aspect of your business.

The first task at hand is to make sure everything, from offices to bathrooms, is kept sparkling clean daily. This says a lot about you and also sets the tone for the property. Prospective clients will assume that this is your standard, and that they are going to be expected to conform to that standard. So clean every day before you open your doors!

Smell. How does your office/recreation center smell? Does it smell stale, or does it smell potpourri-scented? Do not under any circumstances allow any smoking in your center! Post "No Smoking signs" if necessary. Spray air freshener daily or install an automatic potpourri sprayer that releases scents every 15 seconds into the air. One manager I knew hid car air fresheners in some silk trees in the office and in the air vent where the heat and air conditioning blew out of. You can imagine it was very well scented, as those fresheners are extremely strong. Not a bad idea! People respond to smell. It is proven to be one of the strongest senses. Don't underestimate it! Chapter 10 is dedicated to smell, that's how important it is in our industry.

Is the coffee made? The creamer, sugar, and cups out? One company's trademark is fresh popcorn made daily in their company-provided popcorn machine. The smell is wonderful, and you always know when you enter one of their properties because the popcorn is always popped! If you provide cookies, go ahead and set them out. It's a wonderful opening to offer your customers free coffee and cookies when they come in the door, and it makes them feel so welcome. You are so gracious. You are off to a wonderful start!

If you are lucky enough to have a fireplace, go ahead and use it. If it is wood-burning, put logs in the fire and start it. Spend time keeping it going throughout the day. Most of the fireplaces I see in recreation rooms go unused. The reasons are: too much work bringing in wood, watching it, and cleaning it. Then why is it there? When a fire is burning, I've seen people come in the door and stand and stare at the fireplace for minutes on end. I've seen people wait up to an hour for a leasing agent, just sitting by the fire enjoying it. Perhaps it reminds them of a past home or a past memory, or maybe it's just an opportunity to enjoy a good fire. Either way, it brings a wonderful homey atmosphere to your center. So use that fireplace!

Now that we've discussed office atmosphere, let's take a look at offices. Hopefully, you are lucky enough to have two offices, one for leasing and one for management. Remember this...they will come to an OPEN DOOR! The very first door a customer finds he will enter, so if possible make the first office your leasing office. It should also be the most elaborate of the two, as it is the office that represents the property. It should be stocked with the floor plans, office brochures, applications and all appropriate leasing paperwork. It should be uncluttered, with a desk and plenty of comfortable chairs. It should be a relaxed, private office, as this is where your applicants will fill out their applications, and where you will review any concerns they may have. The management office should also be clean, neat and organized, reserved for taking rent payments, as well as solving resident complaints and problems. You can see why we want the two kept separate, as we want leasing to be a positive experience, and resident complaints would intrude on this.

CHAPTER 9: PREPARING YOUR MODEL

Many properties prepare a vacant apartment to show prospective clients their floor plans and how they will look when furnished.

If you have a large enough property you may want to contact a furniture rental company (examples: Globe Furniture, Rent to Own) and very often they will furnish your model free of charge in exchange for business referrals. Of course, the furniture will be more elaborate than most renters own, but I like to refer to this as selling "wishes and dreams." A furnished model properly done will generally bring gasps of "oohs and aahs." This is the effect you are looking for.

Every day when you open your model, have a carpet rake and some of your favorite air freshener stored in one of the closets of your model so they are handy. Give your model a quick spray and rake the carpet so it looks fluffy and new. You may want to install the automatic potpourri sprayers, or the supermarket plug-ins in each room. However, remember to change the cartridges each month with new refills, or you may find yourself with an unpleasant odor when they dry up. Switch on every light you can find and open every drape and blind. Light rents apartments!

If you do not have a model, an excellent way to prepare for showing is to "mini-model" an apartment. This consists of buying some inexpensive items, such as silk plants and a couple throw rugs, and accessorizing throughout the vacant apartment. You can buy designer drape rods and some inexpensive sheer drapes to string through the rods; then add a few silk flowers creating a beautiful drape covering. Over the patio door is a good place to drape, as it is often the focal point when entering. You might want to consider adding an accent wall in a different color of paint, which adds a warm custom-home effect. Add towels, a shower curtain, and a rug to a bathroom, and call it good enough.

For under $100, you can mini-furnish an apartment, and the great thing about this is you can move everything from apartment to apartment as they rent. Check your mini-model every day prior to showing to keep cobwebs down, and spray and rake as you would your furnished model. You could use the air freshener trick in your silk plants. Our staff once rented 39 apartments in two weeks from one mini-model, and never had to do another one. The $100 is a good investment for you because, the sooner you rent up a vacancy, the sooner you can stop showing it—which takes time out of your day.

If you have no other options, please make sure your vacancies smell and look good. Many staff members just won't take the time, and it is so embarrassing to enter an apartment and find surprises. You may also want to check your keys if you are not using a pass key for showing, as many a leasing agent has had to leave their client at the door and return to the office when the keys would not open the door.

CHAPTER 10: Smell and other Senses

Appealing to people's sense of smell has now become a science. Malls are filled with stores that do nothing but specialize in smell. Aroma therapy has become popular.

I cannot overemphasize the importance of smell in the rental business. Real estate agents have long known about the importance of smells in marketing their homes to prospective buyers. A favorite trick is to put a pan of simmering potpourri-scented water on the stove, or put a loaf of bread in the oven on low, so that buyers smell "home" when they pass through the front door. For some reason the apartment rental business has not followed suit, but there's no reason you can't do this on your own.

I personally experienced the importance of smell firsthand. My husband and I were hired to manage a 260-unit apartment complex, and we had to pick out our own apartment. We were instructed not to inform the leasing agent who we were (refer to the chapter on never knowing who your boss will be), and were told to have her show us available apartments, so we could check out her leasing skills. The first apartment had decent enough carpet but the stench was so strong that I had to cover my nose. We politely asked to see another apartment. Unfortunately, they almost all smelled as bad. We finally gave up on looking at downstairs apartments (which is what we wanted, to make moving easier) and asked to see upstairs models. We finally decided on the only apartment that did not have any odor (neither good or bad), even though the carpet was not as nice as in some others. Smell, that's how important it is! With 39 apartments sitting vacant, this was a pretty good clue as to what part of the problem was.

There are some pretty good tricks of the trade in the market now, but few apartment managers or leasing agents will take the time or effort to make them work. They want the apartments to magically rent themselves. Thousands of dollars are spent to make clubhouses and models ultra-luxurious, but very little time is ever spent on the vacant units. Leasing agents tour their clients through these beautiful professionally decorated models, which mislead clients into thinking that this is what their apartment home is going to look like. How disappointing when they turn the key to their apartment and find bare walls and some unrecognizable odor. Who or what must have lived there before them? In this scenario, I guarantee you have a problem before the customer even gets moved in.

Let's look at some ways to avoid these disasters.

First, talk with your carpet cleaner. Many cleaners will inject fragrances into their cleaning water to help insure a nice-smelling carpet. They also carry black lights that can detect pet odor. Ask them to use these. When and if they find a pet odor, they can inject enzymes that actually eat the bacteria. Make sure that your carpet cleaner leaves a window slightly cracked for proper ventilation, and the heat turned up in the apartment to speed the carpet in the drying process. You would think this would be standard practice, but most technicians need to be reminded. If carpets are left to dry with no ventilation they will become moldy, and mold is almost impossible to get rid of. The next day you will want to remember to turn the heat back down, so as to not run up hefty electric bills.

Plug-ins and sprays. The day of your move in, INSIST on doing a pre-check of the apartment—either yourself or your leasing agent. At this time, install an outlet plug-in that sprays out fragrance every few minutes. I like to position it right by the front door so that the fragrance hits residents' noses the moment they enter. Use a carpet sprinkle (I found cinnamon works well, and I have saved thousands of dollars in replacing carpets with this trick). Then heavily spray the apartment with an air spray (I prefer peach, as it makes you feel good too). It is important that you do it the day your client moves in, as the fragrance won't hold as strong overnight. Once your clients get moved into their new home, their own smells will become home, and should any odor occur, they will most likely blame themselves, as the apartment smelled so beautiful when they moved in. It could not possibly be anything else. Believe me, this works. Again, it is just a matter of making the effort.

Also, while you are doing your check, look around for any neglected maintenance. For some reason, maintenance men miss the darn'dest things, such as hanging drapes, no drapes, no curtain rods, no drip pans. You get the picture. You will want to have all this done by the time your clients have shown up for their keys on move-in day. You will not have to worry about being embarrassed about the condition of your rental. It will be perfect, and smell wonderful too.

I always believed that the perfect resident is the one I see on move-in day, and not again until move-out day. They were obviously happy residents.

Good luck and don't forget to pre-check!

Chapter 11: Showing up Early

The early bird gets the worm. This saying really applies in this business. 99% of all managers hired today do not show up until the designated office times posted on their offices or their rec rooms. Usually hours are 10:00 a.m.- 6:00 p.m. Monday through Friday, possibly with some Saturday and Sunday hours. In my experience, I found that I rented an average of three apartments a week by showing up at 9:00 a.m., and took probably three to four calls a day between 9:00 and 10:00 a.m. that I would have missed had I waited till 10:00. People shop early, and if I can get their call before they call another property, most times I can get them to our property and rent to them before another complex even has a chance. If you have the apartment that will fit their needs, they have no reason to look further, nor do they want to, as they have far better things to do with their time. And let's face it, time is money and a very precious commodity in the 90's. Most times on weekends managers have weekend coverage, and here lies another problem. Employees just don't care as much as you do. Most times they are hired on an hourly basis or at a low salary, so they just don't have the same motivation that you do. However, experience shows us that leasing people who earn bonus incentives for each renter are extremely aggressive and motivated, but seldom care who they rent to as long as they can earn that commission. You will need to direct your staff in these matters, especially till you get to that 100% occupancy you are aiming for.

CHAPTER 12: ANSWERING THE PHONE

This may seem like a very simple thing, but it really is not, yet it is your lifeline in the rental industry.

You arrive at your new office, both phone lines are ringing, and you have no idea where the phone is. Where is the hold button? How do I answer the phone?

Let's start at the beginning. As soon as possible you need to get a procedure in place. Find the phone. Find the hold button. What are your phone numbers? You probably have a business number for the apartment community, and what is called a ring-through number. This is a separate line that is used because it bypasses the answering service or machine in case you need to reach the office and these services are in place. You will also need to know whether you have a fax machine, what that phone number is and whether it is connected to your existing phone or on a separate line.

When I start a new job at a new community, I usually place a business card or brochure in front of me and keep it there for a few days, not only to remind me of the community name, but because the phone numbers are handy for quick access.

There are as many theories on how to answer the phone as there are leasing agents and rental companies. This chapter will only give you the basics, but the most IMPORTANT element to remember is to let your own positive personality shine through. DO NOT try to fit any program that insists you follow a strict regiment. Your customer will know and will feel the sales pitch. I remember one job where I downplayed my experience and hired on as a leasing agent on a temporary basis. During my phone calls the manager would be screaming at me across the room things I should ask. Needless to say, I was very embarrassed, and the customer never showed up. At the end of my first conversation with a potential customer, the manager berated me for not getting the customer's phone number. Excuse me, but I myself don't give my phone number out to strangers, so why should I ask this person to?

A good way to start your phone conversation is "Good morning (or afternoon). Whispering Pines, how may I help you?" You might want to take a deep breath and put on a smile before answering. People can sense your attitude even through the phone lines. The customer will most likely ask prices or what you have available. You will want to have all this information in front of you until you know it by heart (which won't take long). Find out when they want to move, and work from that point. If they need a place immediately and you have no vacancies at the moment, then you may want to refer to your sister properties. However, experience now shows most renters are consumer-educated, and start at least 30 days ahead of their planned relocation. This is good news for you. Point out all the positive elements of your property, emphasizing their value, because of course there is no better place to call home than your apartment community. At some point introduce yourself in the conversation with something like, "By the way my name is Lisa, and your name is?" You are establishing a relationship. You will want to invite them out to tour your property. If they are out of state, you will want to offer to send a brochure, application, and a fax number, as it is very possible you will rent to that customer by fax without his or her ever visiting your property. As your skills increase, this will become fairly common. Pay attention as you talk to your customer. You will learn things about the person that will be valuable later on. When they do visit your property, you will be able to pick up on the conversation and they will be impressed that you recall that they work at intel, nike, or wherever. Something will click as you visit that reflects back to your conversation. This again establishes the relationship. They are not just a sale, but a person, a neighbor that you want to live at your property.

Find out how they learned about your property. This is important to companies as they want to know where their advertising money is best spent. Obviously, if there are no calls from the newspaper ad, either the ad needs an overhaul, or the market from the newspaper just is not there, and there is no reason to spend thousands of dollars on a market that does not reciprocate. Your owner appreciates this information.

End your conversation with something like "Thank you for calling Whispering Pines, we look forward to having you drop by to tour." Make sure to give your office hours so you don't miss them!

Good luck with your telephone skills! You will be amazed at what a great sales agent you are over the phone. Remember, BE YOURSELF! You are one in a million.

CHAPTER 13: KNOWING YOUR DIRECTIONS

Many times when you are hired, you are given the keys, and need to move into your new apartment within 24 hours, because you start work the next day. You don't know where you live, let alone know how to tell anyone else your location. You will not have time to find out where you live! The first phone call you will receive on your first day of work inevitably will ask you where you are located. In such cases as these, I have had to resort again to humor "I have absolutely no idea but I'll find out, please hold!" You would rather not find yourself in this situation, so take five minutes before you start answering phones and find out. Unless you have a photographic memory, write down directions east, west, north and south to your property, and keep them right by the phone. You can reread these until they become natural to you. As previously mentioned, know some nearby landmarks, such as stores, schools, etc. Cross streets are important, as are major highways, as well as freeway exits.

Speaking of schools, make a quick list of the elementary, middle and high schools for your residents. Families need to know the schools and whether there are school buses to the schools from their apartment. File a card in a rolodex under "S" for schools for future inquiries.

Take a moment to write down the square footage of the apartments, prices, move-in fees, pet fees or any other applicable information for quick reference. Write it on your community brochure, and in the event you misplace the brochure in a paperwork shuffle, write across the top of your desk calendar for back-up.

Another chapter deals more extensively with your product. This just gives you a fast start!

CHAPTER 14: Greeting and Standing

We have talked about office atmosphere but I feel it imperative to take this one step further. It makes no sense to have atmosphere if there is no one there when the customer enters your open door. I have seen more offices where people come in and look around not knowing where to go. There may be more than one door, so they will just stand helplessly in the foyer, wondering what they should do. The leasing agent and/or manager will stay in their offices and wait for the customer to find them. I have even seen people walk out rather than wait.

The important thing to do is, the second you see that customer coming up the walk, stand and HURRY to meet them. Welcome them to your property, stretch out your hand, and introduce yourself to them. Treat them as importantly as your most wealthy relative, for in one respect they are paying your wages. An appropriate greeting might go like this. "Hi, welcome to Summerhill Estates, my name is Lisa, how may I help you?" The customer feels like they are home, and that's just what you want them to do — rent a home! More times than I can count we have heard customers say they rented from our staff because we were so friendly. We may not have been the fanciest apartments, or even the best value, but they felt wanted and the place felt like home. It is surprising how many properties have cold settings and rude people,

people with attitudes. But this is all to your advantage. So you may not want to share all your secrets!

CHAPTER 15: KEEPING THE DOORS OPEN

When I was growing up, I worked for my mother who was one of the most successful businesswomen that I've ever known. She owned a chain of seven beauty salons, and at a very early age I went to work for her, first sweeping hair off the floor, then graduating to receptionist. Probably the one most valuable trade secret I learned from her was to keep the door open. Before all of the other salons caught on to the wisdom of a "no appointments necessary" policy, she had put this concept into practice. When all the other beauty operators were complaining that there was no business and it was such a slow day that they might as well go home as sit in their hydraulic chairs, she would stay and on most of these days earn an extra $100-$200 after everyone else had gone home. She knew there was no predicting the public. One minute there isn't a customer in sight, and the next, six customers are walking through the door. I have never forgotten this lesson.

I am always the first to arrive, very often the last to leave. Never put a note on the office door that you'll return soon. First off, no one knows when "soon" is, and second, they will not return. The public will go where there is an open door. At lunch time if there is no leasing person to relieve you, even a well-versed maintenance man, or landscaper who can give out a brochure and take a phone number is better than no one. After all, you can't retrieve that customer. Keep those doors open!!!

CHAPTER 16: Marketing

This is probably the most important element to successful resident management, and possibly the most overlooked. Too many managers depend on their property managers, or owners, or just the same old newspaper ad every week to do the trick. They sit on their butts, and complain to anyone who will listen how slow traffic is. I say to these people—depend on no one. "Make it happen!"

I once read of a successful businesswoman who at the start of each staff meeting would have everyone stand up and shout "To be enthusiastic, ACT enthusiastic!" Then she watched the attitude change!

First off, GET ENTHUSIASTIC! Even if you are a staff of one, look at your property and yourself and get excited! You are your own boss, your own marketing director, and you make your business successful. What a challenge, and what an accomplishment!

Let's look at some steps to take.

Take inventory. What does your property have to offer over the competition? Mention these advantages in your description. Location? Use landmarks. Perhaps near the mall, the university, the interstate, centrally located near downtown. Perhaps frost-free refrigerators (low cleaning maintenance), or non frost-free refrigerators (keeps ice cream beautifully). You get the idea!

Cleanliness. Your clubhouse, office and model are

sparkling clean. You represent the clientele you will draw. Everyone likes a clean place, so do some spring cleaning. Your model is opened by the start of office hours and is prepared; your blinds are all opened and all lights are on. No SADD disorders allowed! Light makes everyone feel good, and a happy customer is likely to rent.

Curb appeal. Make sure your grounds are checked daily and trash is picked up. Your current residents, as well as future ones will notice, and appreciate your care. Are your lawns mowed, edged? Are flowers planted? This is your home as well as theirs! Show your pride of ownership.

Personal appearance. Dress as if you are going to a regular office job. This is your job, and you are the boss. Dress like one! Make a memorable first impression! Your image will provide your standards to the future resident who lives in your apartment community. If you are dressing as that 60's love child (again no offense), you are likely to draw that particular clientele. If that suits your property, then point taken.

Now you are ready to meet that potential renter and neighbor. Again, you've hurried to greet your client. Stand up, shake their hand (you can read their body language if this does not seem appropriate), welcome them to the greatest place in town to live! Your apartments!

Enthusiasm! Here's where you'll show and sell your property. Learn their name and give them yours.

Personalize. Everyone likes to be called by their name. Get to know your client as you show your property. Find out why they are moving, what brings them to your area, etc. and fit this into your custom presentation. For example, the client has small children? Well, a playground fits right into your conversation.

Advertising. This is probably one of your most powerful tools. It is also an opportunity to use your creative skills. I never fully understood the power of a newspaper ad until forced to market a 260-unit property with little or no advertising. We ran a 3x5" ad three times a week unlike all our sister properties who had 5x5" ads running daily. After reading the competitors' ads and watching them weekly—one factor became evident! They NEVER changed. These properties were either fully rented up and didn't mind this expense, or were having no luck filling their vacancies. After watching this, my leasing agent and myself came to the conclusion that we should be outrageous with our advertising and do it often. We were not going to be ignored! We created new ads every month (sometimes following a holiday theme). The results were amazing. The liveliness of these continually changing ads made them refreshing and eye-catching. We incorporated the help of our newspaper ad rep, gave her a free hand with the art department, heaped praise on all of them for their talent and watched them go! It got so if we didn't have our ad called in by the first of the month, they called us.

They were ready to use their creativity too. Most clients don't give their advertising reps a chance to use their abilities, so don't be afraid to get to know your ad rep. And remember to thank them for the great job they do! They can be your best ally in a slow rental market. We found we could judge the success of our ad if it was the first one that we spotted when we opened the apartment and rental ads. Experiment, have fun and watch the results!

Never run down your competitor! It's so unprofessional. There will be times when you cannot fit the needs of your customer, but the property across the street can. Well, refer that customer across the street. You may not have rented your apartment, but the customer will remember your kindness and perhaps recommend you to a friend, as you were this terrific helpful person who was more concerned with his or her needs than your own. Word of mouth is your best advertisement! It's been said that a bad word travels 100 times faster than a good word, so we need all the good words out there in the marketplace that we can get.

Go get the business! When calls and clients were slow one week, our staff decided we should go find business. What did we do? We bought inexpensive baskets and filled them with bulk candies, and myself and my leasing staff drove up and down the streets and stopped at every real estate agency along the main thoroughfare. You would be surprised how many real estate agencies there are in your town. We delivered the baskets, thank you notes for future referrals, and lots of business cards. Real estate agents work with people relocating to your area who are between homes, and they need a rental in the interim. Following this strategy, you can meet lots of wonderful professional salespeople who are also happy to meet you (as your renters are probably future home buyers); so they are as eager for your referrals as you are theirs.

Personal advertising. Every person you meet is a potential client, a staple of the real estate industry. So know your community. When I went to enroll my oldest daughter in the airline academy, her counselor and I became friends. I found that even though they had dorm-style housing for their students, quite a few could not fit the criteria for their apartments. Either they had a pet, or were not willing to share one bath with three other occupants, so we were able to provide a service to them by renting to these people who would not be able to enroll without proper housing. These students came from all parts of the country to attend this academy, so this contact turned out to be profitable to both parties. This relationship goes on still to this day; even as we have changed properties, we always accommodate the academy. After our first nine referrals we put together a first-class basket of goodies and delivered it in person to the reps who had sent so much business our way. They were impressed.

We also never failed to send a thank-you note after each referral. Common courtesies like this keep you fresh in their minds.

Beware, however! I made one mistake with this marketing tool. I mentioned it to another person in our business. Big mistake. This person proceeded to contact the academy and offer no move-in fees to their clients if they would send them their way. When I noticed referrals slowing, I contacted my friend who admitted that it had been just too tempting to offer this to their customers. Thank goodness I learned of this and was able to get clearance to offer the same incentive, and we were able to salvage back our account.

Balloons & Flags. Excellent tool. Also a good way to direct traffic flow. Follow the balloons to your spectacular rental center. You may need to get creative here too. One time our competition called us from directly across the street, complaining that business had been slow and asking how many apartments we had rented in the past week. I quietly answered 10, feeling rather sympathetic. The manager replied she simply didn't understand it, so I added humor to make her feel better. "But our balloons are higher than yours." Apparently, their staff took us seriously. The next day their balloons were 22 feet high! As if it were that easy! We immediately flexed our creative muscles and changed the shapes and designs of our balloons so as not to be copying our copycat!

Networking. In time you will meet other managers in the industry. You can help each other with referrals, an especially good tool in slow markets. Be prepared, however, as not all managers share enthusiasm for this concept.

Resident referrals. Some companies offer a gift such as a gift certificate or money off next month's rent for referring others to the apartment community. Residents are usually quite happy to participate in this program. If you do institute this incentive, make it clear to all involved that the prospective renter must pass the screening, as well as move into the apartment in order to qualify for the bonus.

Marketing. Have fun, be creative and outrageous, and market, market, market!

CHAPTER 17: FINDING OUT YOUR CUSTOMER NEEDS

You are a customer-oriented leasing consultant, whether you are the manager or the leasing agent. It is your job to fill your customer needs, hopefully at your property.

First, you want to find out what your customer is looking for. Does he need a one-bedroom apartment, a two-bedroom, a studio? What exactly does this person need? You may be able to downsize him or upscale him depending on the circumstances. Obviously, if he has four children and wants to rent a 3-bedroom apartment, and you only have one-or two-bedroom apartments, you are not going to be able to accommodate him. Find out his needs, and go to work. Below are some examples, and some alternative solutions to your customer's needs.

Say the customer wants a two-bedroom apartment, as he has a lot of belongings. You have no two-bedrooms available, but there is a one-bedroom coming open. You should let him know you have a large one-bedroom, with extra storage built on, and tell him, think of the rent money he will save if he stores his unneeded items, and rents a one-bedroom. If down the road, he finds it is just too small for him, he can always transfer to a two-bedroom. Many properties ask only a fraction of the move-in fees (called a transfer fee) for their residents to transfer to another apartment. This solution many times works well. The same premise holds true for a customer wanting a one-bedroom, when you have only a two-bedroom open. With the small difference in rents of a one-bedroom and a two, wouldn't he like to have the extra room to make into a den, or use for company, or just additional storage?

Say the customer wants a washer and dryer, and you don't have this feature but you do have a laundry room in each building. You might suggest that while you don't have the convenience of the washer-dryer in the apartment, think of the money he will save on the electric bill.

Say the customer wants a frost-free refrigerator and you have only the old fashioned self-cleaning kind. A good way to overcome this one is the ice cream trick. Phrase it this way: Do you know how well your ice cream keeps without all the frost and de-frost going on? Ice cream keeps just great. And look at all the other features we offer. Many times it does not become a major factor.

In other words, find ways to overcome the negative with the positive features, and many times you will find yourself with a new customer!

CHAPTER 18: Pre-qualifying

Real estate professionals understand the value of pre-qualifying their clients. Early in the transaction they will find out their clients' income, and credit history, and whether they can qualify for financing. The reason for this is simple. Working with a customer who won't be able to purchase is a waste of the real estate salesperson's time, as he or she works strictly on commission, and it wastes the prospective buyer's time as well. Time is money.

In the same respect, we need to pre-qualify our clients in this business. They are going to pay you an application fee, which in turn will pay a screening company to determine whether they qualify to rent an apartment. Remember, it is their money. You do not want to waste their money any more than you want to waste their time and yours. Most properties have criteria outlining what qualifications a renter must have. This is true today more than ever, with fair housing laws. Most require that renters' income be three times the rent, that their credit be in good standing, and that they have at least six months' positive rental history and references. Also, a background check is required with most screening services for any felonies. At the end of this chapter I have included sample rental criteria to give you some guidelines.

When you are working with your customer, don't be afraid to ask questions. "Do you have rental history?" "Are you new to the area?" "Are you being transferred in?" "Do you have pets?" "How many people will be living in the apartment?" You will be surprised how much the customer wants to tell you about his or her situation. Positive and negative. If they have a particular problem with a landlord, warning bells should be going off in your head, and you will need to pry a bit deeper without becoming personal. A good rule to use is the third person rule. "Our screening company requires..." whatever you may be discussing. Be careful to never discourage a person from applying, due to fair housing laws. A way to handle this is to say "I'm not sure how the situation you described to me will affect your application approval; however you are more than welcome to put in the application." Most times clients know what is on their report and they do not want to spend $40 or more just to find out what they already know, so this problem takes pretty much care of itself. However, there are a few who think that the system will not find out, and think they will slink right on through. Wrong! Usually when the denial comes back they are not surprised and do not blame you. The biggest problem with "leasing agents" who work on commission is that, no matter what, they want to get that application okayed, hoping that every client will slink on through. Watch for this. When this happens, and you have to turn them down, the clients are generally mad at you because your leasing agent told them they would qualify.

There are special circumstances that will occur, and honesty here is still the best policy. If there is something in a customer's rental history that may cause them to be denied, don't take their application fee and pretend they will probably go sailing through. Say, "I'm not sure how that will affect your application screening, but you will need to find out in any event, so let's go ahead and try it."

Let's go over some of the criteria.

Rental history. Most companies require six months' positive rental history. How do you get rental history if no one will ever rent to you? I suggest to new renters that they may need to have a qualified co-signer to rent their first apartment. Or they may need to pay "first and last month's rent" in order to get started. This is a good time to remind them that, if they pay their rent on time and there are no notices of disturbance, they will not have to ever worry the next time they go to rent an apartment. You are also encouraging these renters to be model residents while they are living under your management, and this will prevent future problems. With a co-signer situation (which follows a separate set of criteria), or a first and last month's rent, you are pretty much guaranteed your rent.

Income. Generally, two and one-half or three times the rent, gross wages before taxes. Roommates qualify together (which makes their income pretty easy to come up with). They may be asked to prove their income with either a paystub or, in the case of self-employment, a copy of last year's tax return.

Credit. A full credit report will be pulled by the screening company. Nothing hides here. If there are credit problems, especially recently, the application will be denied. I predict we will see more problems in this area with the continuing high divorce rate where one spouse leaves the bills to the other to pay. This is a problem we are going to face head-on in a very short time, and new solutions will be needed. Otherwise, a lot of good renters are going to be turned away. We are looking for positive credit history. Three or more late pays will generally result in denial.

Criminal history. Felonies may result in automatic denial. Check with your company, as each has its own set of criteria. Certain time frames or restrictions may apply.

Roommates. These applications are in a special class. The two or three applications qualify together. In other words, their income, their rental history and their credit combine. If one application fails, then it is possible for the remaining roommate(s) to pass and qualify, but doubtful he or she wants to abandon the failed roommate. If the roommates all pass, unless they are blood-related or childhood friends who are used to spending a lot of time together, you can expect that after a couple of months they will have a disagreement and one will want to move out. You cannot, however, discriminate against them in your screening process, and should they all pass I strongly suggest that you add these words as an addendum to your rental agreement in order to protect yourself. "If one roommate vacates, the remaining roommate must be re-qualified and a new contract made." This will save the "I can't pay my rent this month because my roommate ran out on me." You are one step ahead of this story.

Engaged couples. These renters fall under the same guidelines as roommates. Married couples count as one application. This can cause irritation to engaged couples, but due to discrimination laws they must be treated as such.

Remember when you collect the application fees that roommates each have to pay a fee, the same as engaged couples. Only married couples or single applicants will pay one fee. You might also want to insist on a "cash or money orders only" policy on your application fees, as many renters who try to slip through will give you a non-sufficient check, so in case they don't pass they are not out any money. But you will still owe the processing fee. My only concern here is that if you send a renter down the street for a money order, you may lose him to another property. Since you must treat all applicants the same, I usually end up just taking the chance. Losses are not generally high in this area if you have done your job in pre-qualifying.

Pre-qualify. Save time, save money, save yourself a lot of trouble!

CHAPTER 19: SCREENING SERVICES

We have come so far in the last twenty years; so many professional services have come on-line to make the job of resident management much easier. Years ago, after we had shown an apartment, we would have the client sit down and fill out the application, take a deposit to hold the apartment, and send him out the door with a card telling him to call us back the next day with the answer as to whether he was approved or not. If we could not reach a landlord by phone in order to get a rental reference, we could have to call and call back continually (there were no answering machines in those days). We would have to hope the landlord gave us an honest reference and was not simply trying to pass his problem along to us. We would call the clients' employment, speak to whomever answered the phone (there were no human resource departments), and verify his job and wages (the person answering the phone probably did not know the applicant's hire date or the amount of his wages). There were no credit checks ran. There were no background checks for felonies or criminal activity. So we had to make our best judgment with little information. There were no discrimination laws like there are today. Most managers rented by "gut feeling." Not very accurate.

Today, almost all properties have professional screening services to process the applications for you.

Your job is to have the customer completely fill out the application, collect his application fee (usually the amount the screening company charges you), and send him on his way with your card, telling him to contact you in 24 hours with the results from the screening service. You fax the application to the service and move onto your next customer. Very simple.

Within 24 hours you will generally receive the application results, which will fall into one out of four categories.

(1) Approved. No questions here, it could not be better.

(2) First and last month's rent required. Requires applicant to pay a deposit equal to the last month's rent. Usually this recommendation is for minor credit problems on applicant's report, but everything else is good. This deposit covers the last month of clients' tenancy provided proper notice is given.

(3) Co-signer required. Requires a qualified co-signer to sign an agreement to pay rent, should the applicant default on his rent. Check with your company as to requirements for co-signers as they have stricter requirements to qualify.

(4) Absolutely no. A bad application. Never rent to a "No" unless you find the screening service has made

an error. In this event, the applicant will most likely bring it to your attention if he feels there is some mistake. Do not make this judgment on your own, though. Rather, turn the situation over to the screening service to make any necessary revisements. If they change the recommendation, then you can act accordingly.

Once you have your completed screening evaluation back, you will need to inform your applicant. If the terms are agreeable to both parties, you will need to collect the move-in fee or security deposit in order to secure the apartment. This is your guarantee that the applicant is renting the apartment and also the guarantee to applicant that he has an apartment reserved in his name. Your applications should have a statement to the effect that the move-in fee or deposit is non-refundable, should the applicant change his mind after he or she is approved. Check your applications, this is important. The only time you would refund the move-in fee is if you are unable to deliver the apartment in the time-frame stated, which does occasionally occur due to unforeseen circumstances. Should this occur, you might try offering another apartment (if available); otherwise refund his fee. If the renter cancels, you might try offering to apply his fees to another apartment in the near future. Often this will appease the prospective renter, as he does not go away as unhappy about losing his fees.

There is a new concept in the screening industry which is worth mentioning because I believe it is forthcoming. With time becoming so valuable, the companies and communities who comply with this concept will be one step ahead in the market.

It's called the five-minute application. How does this work? The client comes through the door. He or she is generally speaking an upper-end renter, most times an executive who has little or no time to find housing. He may have just gotten off an airplane after having received a job transfer. He's new to your area, and his time is money. He has little patience for spending time even looking at apartments, let alone going through the entire screening process. He or she will be interested in the floor plan, the brochure, and the costs, and will also ask how the neighborhood is, and how close it is to his new workplace. You definitely have the advantage here.

You, being the rental relocation specialist, know all the answers to his questions. And to top it off, you can have his application completed and back within five minutes, as opposed to 24-48 hours, and if he needs to move in right away, that is perfect with you. Why would he ever want to go anywhere else?

This is how it works. The applicant fills out the basic information: name, social security number, most recent address, birthdate, workplace name and phone number for verification. These are the only criteria a screening company needs for a quick screen. We used to code "911" on our applications when we faxed them over, to alert the screening company that this was a five-minute application. Then they would scramble. The applicant must have virtually perfect credit to qualify, and it will be his fault if he is not completely honest. If the client does not meet this criteria, you will need to go with the regular screening process.

Credit can be pulled and analyzed within one minute. It is the experience of professionals in our industry, that if credit is 100% perfect, and well-established, then this is a quality renter that you want. It is rare you will ever have a problem with clients like this as they have spent years developing this credit, and they are not about to ruin it over a rent payment. Most times these customers are home owners, so there is no rental history to check anyway, and their mortgage will show on the credit report. So basically all that is really checked is credit, and within five minutes you have your apartment rented.

The hard part is convincing management companies and owners to go with this service. I think they will find themselves in the dust in due time if they don't follow suit. If I can keep a good renter in my leasing chair, and not heading down the street to an apartment complex where they are happy to do a quick app, I want to do it.

You will want to go ahead and complete the rest of the rental application for emergency numbers, etc. to have on hand in the files. So while you are waiting, you can do his move-in forms and be all ready to exchange rent money and keys when the application comes back 100% approved.

Good luck with this innovative service of the future!

CHAPTER 20: SAMPLE AGREEMENTS

When you are hired with a company, you will go through a hiring process. You will fill out an application, have your background checked, and possibly be tested for drugs. One company that we were employed by required an extensive psychological check. I never knew if we passed or failed or which was required. I only know that after four hours of bizarre personal questions, I really never cared if they hired us or not. It is rare that you will ever go through this process. After all these steps are completed, and you have passed, you will fill out a hiring packet which includes your I-9 and W-4 forms. You will need to have your driver's license, social security card, and green card (if applicable) with you so that copies can be made for your employment file. Any information for medical and dental insurance will also need to be filled out.

Now you are ready to go to work. You will be given a large company packet that will list all the company's policies, plus give you information about their forms, plus state laws. You will need to take time to read all the information, time you may not feel you have. My suggestion here, is to make sample dummy copies of each form that you will need to fill out for when a resident moves in. If you have difficulty understanding the ones in the book, check the files of the existing residents, and hopefully the previous manager did an excellent job with the paperwork. Make a set of copies of these forms as samples, put them in a file, and keep them for quick reference until the forms become embedded in your brain. It will take time to really master these forms. You might want to fill in the parts of the agreements that remain the same (and do NOT require dates or monetary amounts ahead of time). This will save you time and embarrassment filling in the entire agreement while your resident is waiting on you. He just wants to get his keys and get moved in! In my experience, most people never read the agreements that they sign, so it will be up to you to explain what they are signing as they sign. Very seldom do they ask questions, even when they should. I always like to highlight where they need to sign to speed up the process. Often they are signing without reading, trusting your explanation. After each agreement is signed, tear off their copy and hand it to them. If they want copies of forms that do not come in triplicate or duplicate, you will need to make copies for them.

The shortcuts I have mentioned will save you from being overwhelmed in the beginning, as well as alleviate the stress of being unprepared. But trust me—in time the forms will be so automatic, you could fill them out in your sleep.

CHAPTER 21: GUEST CARDS

Guest cards are used at properties for various reasons. These are 5x11"-size cards displayed on the leasing desk that you hand to prospective residents when they enter the door. Ask that they fill them out prior to your showing the apartment model.

A completed card will tell you the client name, their phone number, where they are moving from, how they heard about you (advertising source), how many residents, any pets, etc. It also gives you employment information as well as approximate income. It serves a number of valuable purposes.

First off, you are now on a first-name basis with this person. You also have a source of conversation. If the customer is moving into your area, you could ask "Why are you relocating to our area?" It also gives you the chance to pre-qualify (see Chapter 18). You will be able to point out why this area suits their needs, or why your apartment is great for their children or pet, in general, why this is the apartment for them.

Second, should you not have an apartment available for immediate move-in—and again, most renters shop 30 days ahead—you can file your guest card, and then give them a call when you do have an apartment that fits their time-frame and needs.

Third, the guest card tells how they found out about you, and so you are able to find out where your advertising money is best spent.

Make sure that you create a file for these cards, as they won't do you any good if you can't find them two weeks from now. A file box works great, or if you are computerized, many programs have a template specifically for this purpose.

Use this valuable tool. It works!

CHAPTER 22: GIVE OUT THOSE APPS!!!

Applications are typically very expensive and come in triplicate. Many companies do not like to have you hand out applications to prospective residents because they are so expensive. Many overzealous leasing agents and managers have given out hundreds of apps over the years creating great expense to the property owner. A lot of pressure is put on leasing personnel to "close" at the time they show their prospect, but I personally do not believe that high pressure sales work, so I object to this practice.

I believe that it is important to give out apps with your apartment name filled out at the top and your business card stapled to them (so not to get lost in the shuffle). The reason is that MOST communities are not doing it, and when your shopper goes home he may not remember all the apartment homes he shopped, but he will have your application in front of him. Many times after an exhausting home hunt, prospective renters will think to themselves that since they have your application with them all ready to fill out, they may as well complete it and rent at your community, and get the ball going. End of hunt!

The SECRET here is to make copies on your copier of your company application and use these for handouts. One sheet of legal-size paper costs approximately three cents. Save your expensive applications for the clients who do want to submit an application on the spot.

The objection you might receive from your company here is the handout is not in triplicate. All you need to do is list the client name on an original triplicate and write in "SEE ATTACHED APPLICATION" across the form and proceed with the rest of the agreement (usually the actual rental agreement is listed at the bottom of the application).

Pretty cheap advertising!

It is always a pleasant surprise when in two or three days, or perhaps weeks or months later, one of your apps come back. You never know when you'll be renting an apartment. This also brings an element of excitement to your job—especially when they tell you they shopped all over and this simply is the place to rent. They have their app and fees in hand, and you have rented an apartment in five minutes.

Speed leasing!

CHAPTER 23: ACCOMMODATING DATES

I have yet to figure out why it takes two weeks to a month for some managers to get an apartment ready for their prospective renter. Haven't these folks realized that this is their customer, and if they don't accommodate him, he is going to go somewhere else where they can? Without customers, managers do not have a job, because without rents coming in, there are no salaries going out. Yet this is the single element that I most often fight over with new managers. They say it is just impossible to get an apartment ready any sooner. But the math doesn't add up. It takes one day to paint a one-or two-bedroom apartment, mostly depending on the ceilings and types of ceiling (vaulted do take a bit longer). It takes one day to clean the apartment, and one day to do routine maintenance and clean the carpets. Three days, tops.

Daily loss of rental income can amount to enormous amounts of money if apartments are allowed to remain vacant. If your state has a law that only allows renters to give their notice for the end of the month, then you may want to allow a few extra days on a couple of units, depending on how many you have (such as eight or more). The reason for this is the scheduling of your vendors since they can only work in one apartment at a time and you will need to coordinate accordingly. Many times one or two renters will move out before the last day of the month, which gives you an extra time boost, but you are not able to count on this. If your state allows a resident to give a 30-day notice any time of the month, then the three-day turnover time works great. I like to call it a "three to five day window" to prepare the apartment, and that is how I do my scheduling. This way, I know right when my new resident can move in, and he can set his plans accordingly. We have even done a one-day turnover in emergency cases, which is a bit stressful, but certainly not impossible if it means keeping our customer.

Be prepared for grunts and groans from your staff, but remember, you are the captain of the ship, and your staff looks to you for guidance and direction. Your "can do" attitude is what will direct and inspire them to believe they "can," and they will feel quite proud when all is said and done. You have not asked them to do anything you yourself have not done. Remember that they would be managers if they realized their potential, but the truth in this industry is that many do not want this responsibility and it takes many cogs to make the wheel go around. If one member of the team falls down, we all fall down!

CHAPTER 24: MOVE-IN PACKETS

Organize your move-in packets in the resident's file prior to move-in. Have all your paperwork ready for signature. I like to highlight where residents sign. Explain the forms as you go, have them sign, give them their copies, collect their rent, issue keys, and 10 minutes later they are on their way.

What is in a move-in packet?

Application. The original rental application, the returned screening report, a copy of their driver's license or picture I.D., a copy of their social security card, and a copy of their current paystub (if required by the screening company).

Rental agreement. Fill this out completely with dates, rental amounts, late fees, or whatever your company requires of you. Make sure both you and all residents sign. Your signature as landlord binds the agreement. Give a copy to the resident after completion.

Addendums. Any forms added to the original lease that make adjustments to the original agreement, such as changes in late fees or polices such as the "No cash" policy.

Pet agreements. These forms state the type of pet, its size, name and description and any financial obligation for the pet (pet fee or additional rent for keeping a pet). A good idea to follow: if the resident has no pets, write in "NO PET" in bold letters across the agreement and have them sign. Then if you see "Fluffy" in the window three months later, you can refer to this agreement, write a pet violation and collect the appropriate pet fee. Some communities conduct "pet interviews" for pet approval as well as take a Polaroid picture for the file. This is also an excellent idea in the event the pet is lost. It could prove useful in trying to find the animal.

Rules and regulations. These pertain to standard apartment living rules. They usually are quite extensive as they must be thorough enough to cover all apartments generically, so be aware that some specific rules may not apply to your community. You may have to explain this. To shorten this procedure, I usually have them sign the form to show they received it, and have them take the form home to review, as they will rarely want to spend 10 minutes reading it.

Pool and rec rules. These forms explain the hours, rules, and state laws governing your pool, rec room, spa, etc. Residents sign and date this confirming that they have reviewed and understand them.

Sunbed tanning regulations. This form explains how scheduling of your suntan bed (if applicable) works, as well as safety issues. Have the resident sign a disclaimer stating that he or she fully understands the risks of suntan beds, and takes full responsibility for any health complications that might arise from exposure.

Check-in/Check-out form. This form states the condition of the apartment at move-in. It generally lists that the smoke alarm works and that the residents' have been instructed how to test it. It also states that all essential services are operative (plumbing, electricity, hot water, heating). You will want to do a walk-through with your resident, listing any damages in the apartment in order to protect them at time of move out, and checking the smoke detector with the resident present. Have the resident sign and date the form, and give him or her a copy. Some managers videotape all damage to the apartment at move-in, with the resident present.

Repair and replacement charges. A list of possible charges for damages to apartment caused by resident. This makes the resident liable for such things as holes in the wall, carpet damages, broken light fixtures, etc. Have residents initial and date this, indicating that they understand their responsibility.

Post office and change of address cards. The Post Office will provide these for you to give to residents. This saves a trip to the Post Office for residents and insures they are registered with the postman.

Address and information sheet. A form that apartments can draft giving the resident his or her complete apartment address, phone numbers for utilities, phone service, and school district information, as well as any pertinent community information.

Parking stickers or carport/garage agreements. Explain all parking procedures such as the number of parking spaces allotted. Issue stickers if applicable, register vehicles if this is your policy, and sign any monetary agreements for rent of carports or garages.

Coupons. Many times apartments issue coupons that vendors such as pizza companies provide. These are usually appreciated.

Copy of your community newsletter. A good time to include a copy of your latest newsletter. It makes new residents feel a part of the community, as well as keeps them abreast of events and information current to your complex.

Keys. Don't forget the keys. Usually, issue two apartments keys, one mailbox key, one recreation room key. The resident can make additional copies. Keep one complete set for the apartment key box in the event the resident loses the key or locks himself out.

After all the forms are signed, and rent has been collected, don't neglect welcoming your new resident to his new home.

Chapter 25: Don't Take Cash!!!

This does seem strange, doesn't it? In a world of bad checks, stolen credit cards, and all kinds of scams, it does seem odd.

The number one reason properties do not take cash is your security. If a property is known to take cash, it does open you up to robbery. Think of the thousands of dollars you take in. This certainly could be tempting to a potential thief!

Another reason is personnel. Some personnel are less than honest. This simply removes the temptation.

Carelessness. Many a move-in fee has been found in an envelope in the trash, with the cash safely tucked inside.

Checks are simply easier to replace or trace, should one become lost.

The question now of course is "What about the habitual bad check writer?" After one or two bad checks from a resident, you should make it a policy to accept money orders only. Some supermarkets charge as little as 25 cents for a money order, so you'll be able to overcome the objection of these people who complain about the inconvenience.

The only time I would recommend taking cash is if you know you will not get the money any other way, and then make a quick trip to the bank. This is your decision, at your discretion.

CHAPTER 26: FLUSHING 'EM OUT

It is the manager's responsibility to collect the rents. Each company has its guidelines. Most times rent is due on the first day of the month, and is considered late after a three-to-five day grace period. After the grace period has expired, a notice is issued according to the state guidelines. In Washington, for example, a "Three-day notice to pay rent or vacate" form is issued, giving the resident three days to pay rent and late fees or else vacate the apartment. If the resident does not respond, it can be costly, not only in rent loss, but in court and attorney fees as well. Many managers resort to this practice immediately upon expiration of the notice. There is a trick or two that can save you a small fortune in lost income from these unresponsive residents. I call it "flush'em out."

After the 72-hour notice expires, a great way to find out if the resident is still in the apartment is to place a 24- or 48-hour notice (depending on the state you live in and whichever applies) on the door telling them that you intend to come in to "inspect for vacancy." Some states allow a 24-hour maintenance inspection to be posted for the landlord to make such an inspection, and this will also work. The point is you are coming in! Most residents do not want to see you or have you in their apartment, since they owe you money. Most of the time you will receive a phone call the same day letting you know they are still there and telling you just when you can expect the rent. If they have skipped, you will find out; otherwise you are losing valuable time and rent money by not knowing. It also saves you hundreds of dollars in court costs because if the apartment is vacant you do have the right to take possession (check your state statute). A word of caution here, however: if you do find some furniture and valuables and you are sure the resident has abandoned the property, be sure to follow the procedures for property abandonment for your state. You will also have to determine what is value, and what is garbage, because you have the right to haul the trash out. Should you find the apartment vacant, you will want to change the locks immediately, so as not to allow access back to the resident; otherwise you start all over again.

Sometimes when I issue the non-payment notice, I also attach the entry notice at the same time in order to speed things up. Be aggressive! After all, they owe you money, and it is your job to collect it!

Another trick is to contact the power company. Residents who skip may not pay you, but they generally contact the power company and take the utilities out of their name. If the meter is "red-tagged" for non-payment, you can be fairly confident the resident has moved, unless they are living by candlelight.

You might even want to contact the emergency number on the application, as you consider not being paid an emergency, and inquire if the relatives have knowledge as to whether the resident has moved. This works especially well with younger residents, as they do not want to mess with "Mom." Mom has helped us get plenty of rents paid, most likely because "junior" may be moving home!

Again, check with your company for regulations to make sure you are in compliance, as there are variances in each state. If you are able to use any of these shortcuts, you will save time and money!

CHAPTER 27: SECURITY

It is very important to follow privacy laws. When your resident rents from you there is a trust factor. That apartment is his or her home, and as manager, you need to honor that trust. No one except the people listed on the rental agreement are ever to be allowed access to the apartment. If someone is locked out, you must make sure that the person locked out is who he says he is, and his name is in fact on the rental agreement. Check his I.D. or driver's license. In the event, and this happens very often, his wallet is locked in the apartment, and there is not a copy of his license in his file, a very easy way to check his identity is to ask his social security number. If he knows it, he most likely is that person. Check with your company for their policies on this matter.

In the event that sister, brother, mother, father come to town and say that Johnny says it is okay to enter but you have no verification from the resident, do not give access. Many times the relatives will be upset at first, but will thank you later for protecting their family member's security. Sometimes people do not want their family members in their apartment. You can try calling the resident at his or her work number listed on his application and see if you can get verbal permission, in which access would then be okay, but do not give out the key. Use your master so they do not have a key permanently.

You might run into what is called a "welfare check." Mr. Employer comes to you and says "Johnny has not shown up for work today, he seems depressed, could you go in and check to make sure everything is okay?" The answer is "No." The way you would handle this is to have this person contact the police department who in turn will send over an officer. You are allowed to open the door for the police. In almost every case, everything is fine (if it were not, you would not want to be the one to open the door anyway).

Under no circumstances should you give out keys or open the door. The only exception to this rule is if the resident has filled out and signed a permission slip for you to enter for, say, a maintenance request. Always when your staff enters an apartment for maintenance, have them knock loudly first, then if no response, open the door, loudly yell "maintenance" or "manager," whichever is the case, in the event the resident is in the shower and does not hear you. This has happened many times to maintenance and it is an embarrassing situation. Avoid it if possible.

While we are on the subject of "security," be very careful to not quote that word to your residents and prospective residents. Many will ask if you do have "security," and unless you actually do have a security service on your site, avoid ever using the word. It implies that you do have such a service which may make you liable in the event their car is vandalized, or their apartment is broken into. We know this is outrageous, but people want to blame someone when these things happen, and you do not want to be the target. Your response to the question about "security" should be "No, we have the police and fire department like everyone else." If you know the police or fire department is very close by, you could actually use that as a selling point in your leasing presentation.

Very often prospective clients will ask how the neighborhood is or whether you have any problems. Hopefully, the neighborhood problems are minimal. I think it is important to stress that it is the 90's, and we all need to be proactive and responsible for the neighborhoods in which we live. Hopefully all your residents are in cooperation with you to keep your community a safe place to call home. Some communities have "neighborhood watch" meetings to help prevent crime. You might want to consider this if you do have a crime problem. Police and neighborhood watch officials, however, do not particularly like to work with apartment complexes one on one. The reason is that there is so much moving activity that it is almost impossible to monitor. Few people know their neighbors these days, and many calls could be wasted on innocent people who are moving out and not "stealing" the furniture. So this venture would mostly be up to managers to work out with crime prevention people. Police departments now give seminars for managers, and these can be helpful in teaching what to watch for and how to handle potential problems.

Residents look to you to help keep their neighborhood a safe place to call home. You do so many things for your community, that sometimes it seems no one notices, but in the long run they do notice, especially when rental referrals come your way from people who live in your community and tell others what a wonderful place it is to live!

CHAPTER 28: Youth Careers

My 16-year-old daughter felt it was important that I address younger people in particular, introducing them to a type of career not usually recognized in the school system. So this chapter is dedicated to the younger generation.

Why would young people want to consider this type of career? As a part-time job this offers a great opportunity for students to continue their college and still provide income. Many smaller campus apartments hire a student for a manager in exchange for free rent. With rents at an all-time high these days, this is a major incentive. Also, hours can generally be worked around a student's schedule, and since a student needs to be home to study, this is a win-win situation for both owner and student.

Leasing. Leasing agents typically make $9-$10 per hour. The leasing agent's job is to rent apartments. Many properties also offer bonus commissions per apartment rented (generally $10-$50). An apartment also may be provided as agents may be required to live on site. Medical and dental insurance is often provided. Week-end work is usually required, but no evening hours. Wages vary dramatically from one company to another, so do a thorough job search. For this position you need strong people skills and must be customer-service oriented.

Painting. This may seem a minor career choice.

Many properties hire on-site painters to paint their apartments. Wages are generally minimum, but even this position may provide an apartment. Experience does not need to be extensive, but should skills become refined, it is a very easy to obtain a painting contractor's license (check your state requirements) and become your own boss and charge accordingly. Painting contractors make very good money. Hours are daytime as you need to be able to see. Generally Monday through Friday.

Maintenance. If you have handyman skills, this also might be a career choice. Many maintenance companies are started by persons who have worked in maintenance at apartment complexes. Maintenance persons, once they are in business for themselves, usually charge anywhere from $25-$40 per hour. On-site maintenance persons make approximately $9-$12 per hour, again some with housing provided.

Property management as a career choice is a viable career. The best property managers invariably are those who started at the bottom and worked their way up (in on-site positions). They have the best working knowledge of property management because they have done all the jobs required of the employees, so no feeble excuses given by personnel for inadequate work will get past them. Property managers are the liaison between the owner of the property and the on-site personnel. They are responsible for overseeing the day-to-day operation of the complexes and the personnel, budgeting for the property and keeping the owner informed of all problems or concerns he may need to know about. Their salaries vary from company to company, depending also on experience; but the starting range is anywhere from $20,000 per year, upwards to $50,000+ per year.

CHAPTER 29: SALE OF THE PROPERTY

I feel it is important to address this issue. Many managers give up their careers too soon because of this particular occurrence. If it happens to you, don't be discouraged. It is just business, and in the world of business, everything ultimately has a price.

As little as 10 years ago, it was felt in our industry that "a new broom sweeps clean," and when a new owner or management company took over, generally all of the staff were laid off and all new staff were hired. Managers were taught to go into a property, learn everything they could from the existing staff, then let them go. This kind of tactic was self-serving, bordering on sleazy, and it made the industry unstable, from the manager's point of view. All this has changed now, since various unemployment and discrimination laws have taken effect.

In the event of a sale, do not panic! In the event of a new company taking over, do not panic! It may even work out to your benefit. I can remember our very first year in this industry, when we went through three transitions. Each time it meant better benefits for us. The new companies all offered better medical coverage and more room for advancement, so it turned out to be a positive experience.

Should you not have a positive experience, remember there are many openings in our industry, and you are now a veteran. In a worst case scenario, you can look for another job while you are still employed.

CHAPTER 30: Beware the Clipboard

I have always avoided the use of a clipboard. Managers who walk around with a clipboard seem more like dictators than managers. They stroll up and down making notes and directing staff to do the tasks they themselves do not want to do. You don't want to be this way. You don't even want to risk seeming this way. The best managers are "working managers" who would not ask anyone to do anything that they themselves would not do.

The worst downfall of an otherwise good manager is the "ego." The title "Manager" can easily go to some people's heads. If a manager can treat resident management as a business, which it is, "where the customer is King," he or she will be successful. Yes, there will be times when the customer is wrong. But consider these the exception, rather than the rule, and you'll be a better manager. Be fair, but firm if your customer is wrong. Learn the art of negotiation. Most problems can be solved. A wise property manager once taught my husband and myself that if problems are left for 24 hours, they will often solve themselves. I believe the reason for this is residents will solve their own problems if there is no one else to solve them. But use judgment—if you know you have an emergency, deal with it. The majority of problems are petty and easily solved. It's important to remember that this resident is your customer, and you want happy customers.

Good business spreads throughout your community, and referrals can bring in tremendous business in the future, possibly when you need them the most.

CHAPTER 31: Taking Classes

Take advantage of any free or company-paid education offered. Our industry changes so rapidly with new laws and other information.

For maintenance personnel, many appliance dealers offer free workshops on repair of major appliances. They offer "appliance certificates" upon completion of training, which looks good on future resumes.

Pool companies offer free seminars on pool maintenance and proper use of pool chemicals, as well as providing free water testing to make sure your pool is PH-balanced.

Leasing seminars by keynote "successful" leasing specialists are offered to companies for a nominal charge. Companies are usually willing to pay the corporate charge, as these speakers are especially motivating, and we all need "inspired" leasing agents in our competitive markets.

Managers are usually kept updated by their contract with rental associations, and publications dealing with fair housing legislation. They can also enroll in real estate management courses and attend meetings geared to the resident manager. Check with your company to see what is offered in your area and take advantage of the education provided.

Finally, learn from each other. Talk to other managers and find out what works for them so you can build on their successes in your community. Be willing to reciprocate.

We learn daily in the workplace. Experience is a great teacher, and we learn much from others. Believe that you will always be learning, and you won't ever fall behind in current trends. You may even find yourself "one step ahead" of the competition.

CHAPTER 32: YOU NEVER KNOW WHO YOUR NEXT BOSS WILL BE

The words "Be nice to everyone, you never know who the banker is" stay embedded forever in my brain. They are never more true than in this business.

I have lived the classic Working Girl story. Years ago, when I was a property manager for a large firm, I was responsible for 400+ houses. I needed cleaning people, and my associate had a friend who was in the cleaning business. Since she came recommended, I went ahead and hired her. In a short time I was getting cleaning bills of $200-$250 per unit, which was outrageous. I confronted her and explained that I would not be able to justify such large bills to my owners and tried to reach a compromise. Her response was "Well, that's what it costs." So I chose to hire my own cleaning people and not use this particular person anymore. This in essence put her out of business as I had the majority of homes. A few years went by, and I decided to return to resident managing in order to spend more time close to my children, who were still small at the time. One day I answered the phone and the voice at the other end of the line said, "This is Susan (name changed to protect the guilty), I'm your new property manager, and you are fired!" Apparently, Susan had worked her way up the ladder (the back steps, I am sure) and now my husband and I were her first targets. Keep in mind, we had been with this particular company for nine years. Her motive, of course, was revenge. That never works out, though. This is what happened!

Unfortunately, the owner of the company we worked for had already formed a "secret" task force, and agreed to not interfere with the property manager's business (Bad mistake!), so there was no recourse for us.

But we had lived six years at this particular site, and knew every resident by name. One of our neighbors was a feisty lady who did not take things lying down. (I learned from her the very important lesson I still practice today, that one person can make a difference). When she heard what had happened, even though she had cystic fibrosis, she single-handedly made 90 fliers, walked to each house, and urged the residents to do a call-in protest, not only to the property management firm, but to the owners as well, all between set hours. You can imagine the reaction. That day we had a visit from some of the members of the property management company (not our new boss, however) politely requesting that we make this stop. We explained we had no part in this, it was a private endeavor. We had accepted what had happened, and we were leaving with the two weeks notice that we received, and "bon voyage." Two weeks is not very long to change your life, considering you have now lost your home, all your wages, and all your medical coverage. In addition, you have two small children to feed. It is almost impossible for homeless people to find a job, because they have no phone; in the same respect, it is almost impossible to find a home if you have no jobs. In those days, people did not want to rent to children (which we all know is illegal now). There was no problem with our dog, only a problem because we had children. On the very last day of our notice, we met a lady who lived near our neighborhood who took a chance on us, and we found a duplex to rent. This, however, is not the end of the story.

The property management firm that we worked for had two branches, one in a city 90 miles from where we lived. Unbeknownst to anyone, the president of this branch had been working with the owner of one of their largest accounts to form their own management firm, with himself as president. In this way, the account would save themselves a fortune in management fees. We had known this gentleman for the nine years we had worked for our old company. When he was informed of our abrupt termination by my husband's brother who happened to be working in the same building, he contacted us.

These owners had five local apartment complexes, he said, and he needed someone in our area to manage and supervise all five. Of course we agreed. And who do you suppose the property manager for these five complexes was? You guessed it. Susan! This was her largest account, and now she had lost it to the people she had just fired. She not only lost this account, but within six months, the owners of the homes we had managed for six years were no longer satisfied, and canceled their account also. The last I heard Susan was back cleaning. So the lesson is, be careful how you treat people. You just never know who your next boss will be!

As I mentioned earlier, in this industry, companies send out shoppers (anonymous professionals) to assess your skills and performance; other companies shop you to see how you are doing in the market; and new prospective owners also shop you, which may determine whether you stay on, in the event of a sale.

We once had a ragged, dirty person walk into our beautiful new clubhouse tracking mud. As I was wrestling with the thought of asking this person if he'd mind stepping outside, he held his hand out to me and introduced himself as the new owner of this 206-unit apartment community that we managed. He'd been planting trees at the back of the property, a "hands on" owner. I was so glad I had hesitated.

You never know!!!

CHAPTER 33: NEWSLETTERS

Most managers and staff are terrified of writing a newsletter. We now have companies who will write your newsletter for your property, for approximately $150-$200 per month. I personally oppose this for two reasons. One, cost. It will cost you around $25 per month to publish your own. Second, these services don't know who you are or what the needs of your community are, so their newsletters are completely impersonal. They are filled with articles not even relevant to our industry and are a complete waste of reading time. Residents like to read about their neighborhood. They like to see items of interest to them, about their homes and their lives. A great addition to a newsletter is a classified section where residents can advertise free of charge items they want to sell or purchase, or any services they would like to offer, such as childcare, etc.

It is not difficult to write a newsletter. DO NOT PANIC!!! Take a piece of paper and make a rough draft. Always put a heading at the top of your newsletter which pertains to your property name. If your property name happens to be Bridgecreek, then Bridgecreek News is a perfectly good name for the newsletter. Be sure to list the date of the monthly issue, such as May 1999, and always keep your master for future reference after you've completed your newsletter, or to make additional copies for new move-ins. Address one by one any items that you want to bring to your residents' attention, such as rent reminders. You might write "Rent is due the first of the month, late after the 5th." Be careful to make your newsletter positive. I have seen so many newsletters that sound as if the management is Gestapo and this is very threatening. Do not treat your residents as children. They already have parents! Take a negative and make it positive, such as the previous example regarding rent payment. For example, most companies charge a severe late fee for rent paid after the cut off date (up to $100). You might state: "We appreciate your prompt rent payment on the first of the month as we want to spare you the $100 late charges after the 5th." You get your point across; you reinforce the late charges, but you sound helpful, rather than aggressive.

Other subjects you might want to address are pet policies, parking issues, and lock-out charges. Promote special events such as your pool party, art show, kids' clubs, and future events.

I always like to emphasize that we have a patio patrol, as well as pooper-scooper detectives checking regularly. We have no such staff "per se" but we ourselves are these patrols. Nothing is worse than driving by a property and seeing an abandoned couch or tires on a patio, or blankets on the windows. When residents think someone is checking on this, it discourages these practices.

Artwork. Should you want to add this feature, there are different ways to go about it. It is always nice to follow a theme of the month, such as holidays. Valentine's Day, Christmas, New Years, Thanksgiving. You can paste or glue a sticker of some kind onto your newsletter; a bit childish perhaps, but it does work. Art or hobby stores sell artwork "clip art" books. You can take a copy of a page, clip your selections, then glue away. Printing companies such as LazerQuick sell sheets of artwork very cheaply that you can buy and select to add to your letter. If you have a computer and are lucky enough to have an artwork application, you can do the letter and artwork on the same program.

Take your newsletter to a printing company, have it printed on attractive colored paper and deliver to your apartments. That's not so hard! Residents truly appreciate this. It makes them feel more at home, and they are less likely to go hunting for a new apartment every time they get a pay raise.

Get your newsletter out on a consistent timeframe. I like to have it ready around the 20th of the month with a cut-off of the 15th for residents to turn in their classified ads. That way, it is delivered by the end of the month.

The hard part is getting someone on staff motivated to deliver it. A nice enticement is "We pay you for this aerobic work-out!"

Good luck and have fun with this venture. Use your imagination and your own style!

Chapter 34: Create a Festive Atmosphere

Particularly during the summer months, people are in a partying mood. One particular company we worked for institutes one month during the summer for "Resident Celebration" for the residents of their properties. One week during a selected month, a minimum of three events are planned, complete with a printed itinerary handed out. This is an excellent retention tool. A happy resident is not likely to be out shopping the competition. It also gives something back to the members of your community for all their efforts to make your property a wonderful place to live.

We are going to explore some possible party suggestions for your property. Of course, a lot depends on your budget, your owner, and your energy level.

The pool party! Pretty traditional for properties with pools. Shortly after you open your pool (traditionally opens Memorial Day and closes Labor Day, depending on your state's weather), you will want to plan a pool party. Start early, promoting your party in your newsletters. Perhaps add a banner outside your door saying something like "The party is here!" It gets your residents talking, preparing them for the party, and it is also an excellent marketing tool for your prospects, when they ask you "Where is the party?" And of course they will want to move in before the party starts! You can hire a DJ fairly reasonably if you shop around (that way you have music, and everyone loves to be entertained). Or you may have talent in your apartments looking for a showcase. Our most successful pool party included a resident who was a member of a band. He brought his whole band, including himself dressed as an Elvis impersonator, all free of charge. Neighbors dropped in to see this one!

Barbecue is always a good idea. If you do the barbecue yourself, you will probably want to stick with foods not subject to spoilage. I do not suggest certain meats, due to liabilities. Chips are an easy addition. All you need is a few condiments and paper plates, and you are set. You can contact a soft drink company, and many times they will deliver a pop machine with a selection of fountain drinks (usually up to five) free of charge except for the amount of fountain drinks that you consume. In addition, cups are often supplied. If your property does not have a barbecue, many staff members have barbecues they are happy to lend, and you don't really need many, say for hot dogs which cook so quickly. Usually, when we do hot dogs, we do a bunch ahead, cover them with foil and keep on cooking. You can buy hot dogs and buns at discount stores or meat and bakery suppliers fairly reasonably. I elaborate on the party idea because it is surprising how few people know how to put on a party or are afraid of the venture totally.

Anything that you can do, especially at low cost, is

appreciated. Another idea is an art show. Many artists need outlets, and would be happy to display their work for free. Frequently they are willing to offer your residents the opportunity to buy their art at a considerable discount. Serve cookies and cider and have fun. Your residents will enjoy this event that you took the time to plan for them.

Monday morning madness. This is a particularly cute idea that our staff has enjoyed. On some Monday morning (the most blah day of all for working people), you and your staff stand at the front entrance to your property with coffee, juice and donuts; hand them out as the residents drive by on their way to work. Of course, you may feel a little foolish (we did this on April Fool's Day so at least we had a reason to look foolish), but you'll soon be having laughs, as residents ask what you are doing out here. And of course, it's just because you appreciate them so much. Can you imagine all the free advertising you are receiving when they get to work and tell all their associates and friends what they have just experienced? Well, of course they want to move to this crazy place to live too. There is just not enough fun in this world, and too many properties are simply too serious. Lighten up and enjoy your job and residents!

Midnight swim. One night keep your pool open until midnight. Especially during a hot month such as August when people can't really sleep till late anyway. When we have tried this event, we found most times we had closed by 11:00 p.m. because everyone had finished early. They just loved the idea they could swim until midnight if they wanted.

Continental breakfast by the pool. Saturday morning when most residents are home, throw a continental breakfast with donuts, coffee, and juice. If your budget allows, you can add fresh fruit, muffins, etc. We know this works because every time our family goes to Disneyland, we make a point of staying at the one motel that includes this feature. We just love it and look forward to it.

Book an event. There are many events you can book. White water rafting is popular. The more that book, the better the price rate. "Murder express" is also popular here in Vancouver. You pay $49 which includes a river cruise, dinner, and theater where you are part of solving a stage murder. Each area of the country has its own special events that you can check out.

Pet contest. Children particularly like this one, as everyone is proud of their pets, and it gives children pride of ownership. Prizes could be small cash prizes or ribbons. Categories might include cutest pet, ugliest pet, and the pet who most looks like his or her owner.

Line dancing classes. Have free line dancing classes a couple of nights of the week. If you are lucky enough to find an instructor, that is perfect. If not, buy or rent a videotape. Many people want to learn this popular form of dance, but many times you are required to go to a bar, and for some people this is not an option.

Open houses. These work well, especially at holiday times. On Christmas you can serve a fancy punch and cookies, hold a patio-or-deck decorating contest, and announce the winner at your party. Offer cash prizes for first, second, and third place.

Garage sale for your property. Have one designated day that your residents can have a garage sale. If you have garages and carports, this is perfect. If not, you will have to settle for a designated area. Place an ad in the paper, decorate your property with balloons, and place signs everywhere. Advise the participating residents that they will need to be able to make change if they make a sale. Instant success!

There are as many possibilities as there are ideas. So think creatively and enjoy!

CHAPTER 35: STAFF MEETINGS

If you manage a larger property, take time once a week to bring all your staff together. Set aside one morning, perhaps one hour before regular scheduled office hours; pick up some donuts and serve the coffee.

Set up a structured meeting with a list of points you want to cover. Otherwise it can get into a gossip or gripe session. This is not the objective, and is to be avoided at all costs.

This is a good time to cover any changes in company policy, as well as safety issues. It's also an opportunity to let everyone bring up issues relevant to the property. Everyone has ideas to share, from leasing agent to maintenance person to grounds keeper. Some of the most valuable information may come from the grounds person, as he or she is the one who walks the property daily and sees exactly what is happening. The meeting will also give you ideas and information needed to feed into your newsletter.

Everyone wants to be part of an organization and feel they are a contributing factor in its success. The "team" approach is always the best strategy to success, and it takes every working team member to make a successful site operation. You can compare a team to "dominoes." If one member falls down, we all go down. For example, say a painter does not get an apartment painted. This means the cleaning person can't clean, which in turn throws the carpet cleaner off-schedule, etc. You get the idea. Every member is important. If your company agrees, you may want to consider buying team T-shirts and asking everyone on the staff to wear them one day a week (Fridays work well) to show their team spirit. By the way, it is a good idea for maintenance personnel to always wear some form of company I.D. for security reasons.

You may want to have staff events from time to time. Some pizza companies will donate a couple of free pizzas to a property in exchange for distributing their coupons in your move-in packets. You will probably have to ask, however, as they usually don't volunteer, but remember it is a two-way street. Or you may want to do a potluck lunch together occasionally. Employees who feel appreciated aren't as often looking for other employment, and this helps to keep employee turnover down.

Be team-oriented! How can you not succeed with all this positive focused energy?

CHAPTER 36: WELCOME HOME!

Move-in day has arrived! You have done your final pre-check, which is the most important service you will do for your customer. You have inspected your client's new home prior to opening your office—just in case the client is waiting at the door for you. Now you want to go one step further.

Purchase a small "Welcome to our Community" gift to leave in the apartment. Many companies now specialize in this type of industry. Or if you are creative, you can make your own. For under $5.00 you can purchase welcome gifts such as snacks, toiletries or soaps, complete with a welcome card and a bow.

All in all, if you take the time to care, you will be a successful resident manager. Reputations spread fast in our industry, and as yours does, you will find yourselves in demand, which brings financial and status rewards. Once you are fully accredited, you will find opportunities in our business in almost any state you might want to travel to. There will always be a demand for "resident managers," just as there will always be a demand for housing. What better job security could there be?

Good luck with your new career, and may you find as much personal satisfaction from this career choice as my husband and I have!

Notes

Notes

Notes

Notes

Notes

Notes

Notes

ORDER FORM

POSTAL ORDERS: LODAY PUBLICATIONS
P.O. BOX 2722
VANCOUVER WA. 98668, U.S.A.
TEL: [360] 882-0566

Please send me ___ copies of APARTMENT MGRS. SURVIVAL GUIDE.
I understand that I may return any books for a full refund from 14 days of shipment if not fully satisfied.

Sales tax: please add 7.7% for books shipped WASHINGTON addresses.

Shipping: $3.00 for the first book and $2.00 for each additional book.

Payment: cheque or money order.

COMPANY NAME: _____

NAME: _____

ADDRESS: _____

CITY: _____

TELEPHONE: (_____) _____

THANK YOU FOR YOUR ORDER.

AUG 1 5 2000